THE VISIBLE AND INVISIBLE MONSTER

THE VISIBLE AND INVISIBLE MONSTER

A Woman's Tale of Rape, Panic Disorder, and Finding Her Way Back

MARY SUE MILLER

COOKE HOUSE
PUBLISHING

Winston-Salem, NC

The Visible & Invisible Monster: A Woman's Tale of Rape, Panic Disorder, and Finding My Way Back

Copyright © 2024 by Mary Miller

All rights reserved. No part of this publication may be reproduced or transmitted in any form or by any means electronic or mechanical, including photocopy, recording, or any information storage and retrieval system now known or to invented, without permission in writing from the author, except by a reviewer who wish to quote brief passages in connection with a review written for inclusion in a magazine, newspaper, website, or broadcast.

ISBN: 979-8-9852656-0-6

Cooke House Publishing
(a division of Cooke Classic Branding & Design, LLC)
www.cookeclassic.com/chp
publishing@cookeclassic.com

Published in the United States of America. First Edition

Author's Disclaimer:

This book is a memoir. It reflects the author's present recollections of experiences over time. Some names and characteristics have been changed, some events have been compressed, and some dialogue has been recreated.

Acknowledgments:

My support group

In loving memory of
My husband Tommy
My parents John and Janie
and my brother, James

For my beautiful daughter,
Dr. Dee,
I will always love you.

And for my grandchildren
Tommy and Tyler,
You are my pride and joy.

Contents

Foreword	9
Introduction	11
Chapter 1: The Monster is Born	15
Chapter 2: I'm a Survivor	25
Chapter 3: Life Goes On	31
Chapter 4: A New Start	34
Chapter 5: Moving Forward	39
Chapter 6: My First Apartment	43
Chapter 7: A New Love: Jackson	45
Chapter 8: A New Life: Business School	50
Chapter 9: Am I Crazy?	52
Chapter 10: Starting Over … Again	56
Chapter 11: Keep Fighting	59
Chapter 12: My Next Love: Jesse	63
Chapter 13: Home is Where the Heart is	68
Chapter.14: Midnight Rides: The Monster Rises	71
Chapter 15: To Have to Hold	75
Chapter 16: Seeking Help	80
Chapter 17: Tommy's Secret	85
Chapter 18: Married, but the Monster Lives	87
Chapter 19: My Daughter, Dee	92
Chapter 20: Secret Revealed	98
Chapter 21: Another Doctor	100
Chapter 22: Going Home	104
Chapter 23: Fear of Flying	111
Chapter 24: Saying Goodbye	114
Chapter 25: Michael	116
Chapter 26: The Monster Revealed	121
Chapter 27: You Can Do It	130
Chapter 28: My Daughter Frees Me	136
Chapter 29: Robert	141
Chapter 30: Closure and Forgiveness	147
About the Author	155

Foreword

Mary gives the reader a descriptive account of her long struggle with trauma as a small, rural town teenager through all of her adulthood. She opens up and gives the reader a chronology of her sexual victimization and oppression, victim blaming, mental illness, relationship and family dysfunction. Mary tells her story through journaling her pain, failures, emotional dependency, insecurities, faith, poor self esteem and fears after being raped by a local young man in the community. Mary shows the reader her spiraling emotional decline in her secrecy about her sexual assault and mental illness.

Mary initially shows the reader how her close and trusting family - parents and siblings- sustain her and later on shows how her family along with her husband and daughter sustain her. Mary gives a clear and profound depiction of how her family's love and support turn into dependency and negative reinforcement. Mary shows how she is a fighter in spite of her cruel sexual trauma and debilitating mental illness. She eventually comes face-to-face with her past and figures out how to confront her trauma and mental illness through self empowerment and forgiveness. Mary's resilience starts late, but she finally gets the bounce in life that had always eluded her. Through all of her life struggles, defeats and complexities, Mary called on her faith to get her through life's darkness. Mary attributes her triumph to God's mysterious way with her.

Faye Hardy Bordeaux, LCSW
Licensed Clinical Social Worker

Introduction

Dear God,
I can't take it anymore. I should just take my life, but I don't want to die. Keeping this secret is an enormous burden on me. Please, God, remove this obstacle that is a stumbling block in my path. I desperately need You right now. I'm so afraid, and I want so badly to be just like my siblings and friends. I don't like feeling invisible when I socialize with them. I envy them when they go places and do things I can't do. Please, God, help me.

I wrote this prayer in my journal every day, my eyes glistening with tears. For a long time, my journal was my best friend. It was the only place I could expose my secret and get some comfort.

. . .

In October 2019, I watched Dr. Christine Blasey Ford tell Congress her story of sexual abuse by Brett Kavanaugh. I couldn't hold back the tears that rolled down my face. I could relate to her story. The more I listened to her testimony, the more I realized how similar it was to my own. I'd carried a heavy load on my shoulders for so many years. For most of my adult life, no one knew how much I struggled every day because I was too afraid to tell my secret. The only way I knew how to handle my secret was to have faith in God. I knew one day He was going to answer my prayers.

    I didn't read the Bible regularly when I was younger, but I thank God my parents taught my four siblings and me how to pray. It wasn't until I was older that I became interested in reading the Bible all the way through from cover to cover. Then, I understood it better.

When I prayed about my situation, my mind reflected on God's creation. The creation story is one of my favorite Bible stories because it shows how women and men complement each other. And it teaches us that a woman should not have to struggle with violence, sexual abuse, or being assaulted by men.

For so long, men have continued to exercise their power, getting away with impunity. I asked God why men treat women like objects, but I don't have the answer to that question. After all, a woman is bones of man's bones and flesh of man's flesh. We are their helpmates. God made us in His image and likeness. Male and female.

On the day of Dr. Ford's testimony during Judge Kavanaugh's hearings, I was on the phone with my baby sister Mae. Seeing the time on my nightstand clock, I promptly ended the call because missing the hearing was out of the question. It resonated with me just like it did for thousands of other survivors; it led me to speak out for the first time.

I raced against the clock to finish my morning routine. The only thing left for me to do before I got comfortable was caring for my second grandson, Tyler. He had just turned three months old. My five-year-old grandson, Tommy—who is named after my late husband—was at daycare. I love caring for my grandchildren. Although it can be challenging, it is also rewarding. I was astounded when I first noticed that Tyler was the spitting image of my late husband. I frequently mentioned that Tyler should have been the one named after him instead of his older brother.

That day, I went to the kitchen and made myself a cup of hot tea before going to watch TV in my bedroom where Tyler was sleeping. It was a perfect time for my grandson to take a nap, and I appreciated the quietness of my bedroom. I could focus on watching Dr. Ford give her opening statement to Congress with no distractions. Often, I walked across my bedroom floor to check on Tyler sleeping in his bassinet. He smiled in his sleep. I needed to see his sweet face because my anxiety was getting the best of me.

I applauded Dr. Ford for taking a stand for women worldwide. She shared her story with Congress about the alleged sexual assault by

Judge Kavanaugh. Instantly, her story caused an emotional flashback to the dreadful night I experienced sexual assault.

Dr. Ford stated in her testimony that she could not remember every detail that happened to her. Neither can I.

...

The "Me Too" Movement inspired me to tell my story. It has raised awareness of the pervasiveness of sexual abuse and assault in our society today. Some men do not realize that women do not appreciate being belittled by their irrational behavior. The "Me Too" movement awakened my eyes to realize that we had accepted this culture of demeaning women for centuries. We'd accepted it by saying things like, "boys will be boys" or placing the blame on women for being at the wrong place at the wrong time. We urged women to dress modestly and avoid certain male relatives because "that's just how he is." Sexual abuse and assault can be devastating and humiliating and often lead to substance abuse, suicide, psychiatric disorders, and anxiety disorders.

For years, I had dealt with unresolved psychological issues that had caused me not to have a productive life. Unknowingly to my family and friends, I was suffering with unexpected feelings of intense fear and anxiety, constantly thinking my life was in danger. I was depressed and had moments when I didn't want to live. I had low self-esteem, no self-worth, and struggled with social anxiety. The visible monster, Robert, heavily affected me emotionally. I suppressed my feelings for many years. No one knew how much the visible monster had taken over my life. My sadness had turned into anger and my anger turned into bitterness. The visible monster had gotten away and there was nothing I could do about it. I had lost trust in everyone. The reoccurring nightmares would always be a man with a gun trying to kill me. I would wake up with heart palpations. It was like a drum beating in my chest. I couldn't breathe and felt like I was being smothered. When the visible monster showed up on my dates, I had flashbacks to that dreadful night. The traumatic experience causes a lot of pain and suffering for so many women, and sometimes it never goes away.

Telling my story has helped lighten my heavy burden. It has caused me to speak out for the first time. My story will shed light on anxiety, panic attacks, and claustrophobia, which often go unnoticed and untreated.

Anyone who has gone down this dark road, after you read my story, you will see you're not alone. Speak out! There is a light at the end of the tunnel!

The Monster is Born

I barely knew the Monster. (I called him Robert because for a long time that's what I thought his name was.) I had seen him at school, but I'd never had a conversation with him and didn't know his age. Robert was a junior in high school, and I was a senior when I had an encounter with him. However, I will never forget the feeling that came over me when I saw the gun in Robert's hand and realized my life was in danger. I had never been that close to a gun and seeing the monster pointing it at me was terrifying. My life flashed before my eyes. Without a doubt, I felt any minute he was going to pull the trigger and shoot me if I didn't obey his command. I thought I was going to die. Fear paralyzed me. I couldn't move, speak, or cry out for help. He forced me to lie down in the back seat of the car that was parked under a large tree at an unfamiliar place of the highway near my home. I tried to do everything he requested. His rage was evident as he screamed, "Pull off all your clothes! Now!" He repeatedly threatened to kill me if I did not obey his commands.

During the time he attacked me, I laid there powerless, trying to stay calm. He took complete ownership of my body and forced me into sexual activity that I had not consented to. What was doubly horrifying was that my friend's sister, Dorothy, Roy, and Roy's cousin were standing outside the car, watching and waiting while he raped me. When Robert touched me, my chest tightened, my stomach tied in knots, and my body went into shock. My mind couldn't comprehend what was happening to me, and the pain was indescribable.

After Robert raped me, he had a grin on his face as if he had just hit the lottery. Dorothy and his friends were standing beside a tree when Robert got out of the car with the gun still in his hand. He demanded that everyone get back in the car. I wanted to ask someone to help me, but he threatened to kill anyone who didn't do what he said.

I don't remember what Robert did with the gun when he got back in the car. He sat in the front passenger side seat as I sat in the back seat near the window behind the driver. Dorothy sat between me and another guy I had never seen before was on the other side. Everyone was silent except for me. I sobbed uncontrollably all the way home. Guilt, anger, shock, and shame tore through me, knowing that three people had watched me undress and waited while Robert raped me. Traumatized and disoriented, Robert's friend couldn't drive me home fast enough, where I knew I would be safe and secure.

Still crying profusely when I got home that night, I went straight into my parents' bedroom. I woke them and told them what had happened. They simultaneously jumped out of bed. My mother ran to me and held me tightly as I told them I had been raped. All I could think about while the monster was raping me was my parents. I screamed inside, wanting them to come to my rescue. I was confident that my parents would believe me when I told them what happened and that they would be there for me. I'll always remember how they looked when they saw me. It was like they had just awakened from a horrible nightmare. They seemed terrified when I said Robert had a gun and threatened to kill me if I did not obey his commands.

Immediately, they asked me questions about him I did not know how to answer: Who was he? Where did he live? What did he look like? The only thing I thought I knew about him was his name. They wanted to know how that attack could have happened when I'd gone out with my trusted friends.

...

I love my friend Lee Anne, but I'll forever regret that she asked me to go out with her and her boyfriend, Don. When she picked me up, one of her younger sisters, Dorothy, got in the car and tagged along with us as we were about to leave. Lee Anne and her boyfriend dropped Dorothy and me off at the Red Rose Club. She didn't say where they were going. I just assumed she wanted to be alone with her boyfriend because she often went off with him alone when we went out together. Until that night, she'd always returned to the club and joined us before it closed. That was why I believed her when she said she would be back shortly.

Back in the day, the Red Rose Club was in Greenville, North Carolina. Greenville had a population of less than one hundred thousand people and was about six miles from my hometown of Simpson. Everyone in the surrounding areas went to Greenville to shop for food and clothing. Going to Greenville was a big deal. Most people would dress in their best clothing just to go shopping in Greenville. I looked forward to going to Greenville in the summer to shop with the money I earned working on Mr. Hauge's tobacco farm. Out of the $25.00 I earned weekly, my parents gave me a weekly allowance of $5.00. Even though it was not enough money to buy clothes, I was eager to go shopping in Greenville and have fun with my cousins and friends.

Most of the young Black people in Simpson went to Greenville to have fun at the different clubs. The Red Rose Club was one of the most popular places. I'd often go there with my cousins and friends. The club was on the second floor of a small building. Most of my friends and classmates went there to dance and have fun. The first time I saw a jukebox was at the Red Rose Club. It fascinated me that I could put a nickel or a quarter into a jukebox, and it would play my favorite songs.

In high school, my friends teased me for being a wallflower because I never liked to dance in front of people. I enjoyed dancing, and kept up with all the latest ones, but I was too shy to dance in front of people. Once, my cousin Davy forced me onto the floor to dance with him. Everyone was in awe to see me on the floor, dancing for the first time. Knowing everyone was watching me made me more fearful. I never got the courage to dance again.

...

Lee Anne and Don didn't return to the Red Rose Club that night as they had promised, leaving Dorothy and me stranded without a ride home. As the club prepared to close, Dorothy and I frantically searched for a ride home from those leaving in their cars.

When Roy came out of the club, he saw Dorothy and me anxiously standing outside near the club's door. He asked why we weren't leaving like everyone else. The desperation in our voices drew his attention. We told him that Lee Anne and her boyfriend never returned after dropping us off, so he offered us a ride home. We knew Roy because he attended the same school we did. Also, he was in my younger brother's class, and we visited some of the same churches in the surrounding area. He was always a nice person, joking and laughing with everyone every time you saw him. There was no doubt in our minds that we could trust him to take us home safely. Well, that's what we thought.

It didn't bother Dorothy and me that Roy had his cousin and Robert with him. Back then, most people didn't have cars and often caught rides with friends. Cars would become overloaded with more bodies than seats. That night was the first time I met Roy's cousin. He appeared to be around our age. When Dorothy and I climbed into Roy's car around 11:00 p.m., we expected to go straight home. Dorothy and I sat in the back with Roy's cousin. Robert sat in the front, on the passenger side. About three miles from where I lived, I noticed Roy turning off the main highway onto an unfamiliar dark road I'd never been on before. I had no clue where Roy was taking us.

Most sexual assault survivors don't remember every detail of what happened to them. I don't remember the date or the month; I only remember a spring or summer night. It was pitch-dark, and there was no one around. I had no idea that riding home with Roy would turn into a living nightmare. If we would have had mobile or landline phones, we could have called my parents or someone to come and get me.

Dorothy and I expected something terrible would happen as soon as Roy turned off the main highway. Simultaneously, Dorothy and I raised our voices, screaming, "Where are we going?" Of course, Roy knew the right way to Simpson. He had visited our town more times than I could count on my fingers. Roy lived about six miles from Simpson. Both our towns were small communities. Simpson was primarily a residential town. The high school near Simpson that Black people could attend was in Grimesland, and that's where I'd become acquainted with Roy, who lived there.

Roy pretended to be oblivious to Dorothy and me repeatedly screaming, begging, and pleading with him to take us home. He drove a short way down an unfamiliar road to a remote area and parked his car under a large tree. To this day, whenever I ride or drive on that highway and approach a large tree, I have a flashback to that dreadful night. I often wonder, *Is that the tree I was under the night Robert raped me?*

I was shaking and trembling uncontrollably in a fight-or-flight reaction. I tried to be calm and counteract my increasing anxiety; maybe it was just a joke. Nothing terrible is going to happen to Dorothy and me, I thought. Robert didn't say anything until after Roy parked the car. Then he got out on the passenger side of the car and pulled out a gun. I saw the fear on everyone's faces when Robert pointed the gun at us. He told everyone to get out of the car except for me. After the rape, I felt dirty. Filthy. No matter how many times I took a bath, I could never make the feeling go away. I had never seen my parents express intense anger toward anyone in the manner they acted toward Robert. A fierce look arose across my father's face. How badly he wanted to go to Robert's house that night to confront him. However, he had no transportation, telephone, or way to contact him. All the commotion in my parents' bedroom woke up my siblings. Everyone was listening to me explain what had happened. When I described Robert to my parents and told them he was one of my brother's classmates, my brother was furious. My brother told me he was the type of person who would do something like that. He forced women to have sex with him and then brag about it to his classmates like it was no big deal.

We were up for the rest of the night. When I went to bed, I couldn't sleep. I didn't want to think of what had just happened to me. I felt ashamed.

My brother told my father where Robert lived. He didn't waste any time the next morning trying to get to Robert's house to talk to his parents about what happened. Since we didn't have a car at the time, my father got his nephew, Isaiah, to drive us to Robert's house. Isaiah always had one of the most beautiful cars in Simpson. He kept his car looking as clean and shiny as it was when he bought it. Only a few other people in Simpson had cars.

Barely saying anything, I sat in the back seat with my mother during the fifteen- or twenty-minute ride to Robert's house.

The house sat close to a highway, surrounded by woods. Robert's mother was sitting on a chair on the back porch, alone. I assumed Robert was inside the house. When his mother looked up and saw my parents, she had a surprised look on her face. She thought my parents were there for a visit. Back then, visitors would just come to your house unannounced. By the way they embraced each other, I realized my mother knew Robert's mother. It turned out they are cousins, but I had never seen her before. I knew cousins who lived in Simpson and Greenville.

My mother didn't waste time with any chitchat. She immediately told Robert's mother the reason for the visit. Shock spread across Robert's mother's face when I said her son had sexually assaulted me. I told her he had a gun and threatened to kill me if I did not follow his commands. I thought she would go into the house to take him outside so my parents could confront him about what happened. Instead, she looked at my parents and softly said, "He's not home." He had just left to run an errand with her husband. I can't remember all that she said to my parents, but I remember she didn't defend her son for what he did to me. She was apologetic and repeatedly said, "I'm sorry," to both my parents and me. I often wonder if she knew her son was that kind of person because she never said, "I don't believe you." She just kept saying how sorry she was for what happened to me.

Flushed and nervous, she timidly asked my parents what they would do about what had happened. My father said he was going to report Robert to the law. Robert's mother begged and pleaded with my parents not to involve the law. She called my mother by her first name and said, "Jane. Please do not call the law. If your daughter is pregnant, I'll take care of the baby." When she said the word "pregnant," that was the first time it dawned on me that I could be pregnant. *Oh God, no. That is the last thing I want to happen to me. I don't want to have a baby by this monster.*

Immediately, my father disregarded what she said. He wanted Robert to be punished for what he did. I couldn't believe Robert's mother was trying to bargain with my parents. It was like a slap in the face that she thought raising a potential baby from her son's violent and vile act would solve everyone's problems. She didn't understand that my parents wanted him punished, and if I were having a baby, my parents would have dealt with that later. "No deal" was my father's final decision.

We waited for what seemed like hours for Robert and his father to return from their errands. Finally, Isaiah said he had to leave. He had other plans for that day. I looked at my parents with tears welling up in my eyes; I desperately wanted my parents to confront Robert. It was almost like having the nightmare all over again.

My father took the law into his own hands. He wanted Robert punished right away. So, he and I talked with Dorothy's mother. She was a kind woman. Everyone in Simpson admired her personality.

The day my father and I went to Dorothy's mother's house to talk to her about having Robert punished, she just assumed we were there for a visit. She offered my father and me a chair. My father refused to sit. We both were standing beside each other when he told her what happened. Dorothy's mother and I were astonished and shocked when she told my father that Dorothy had not mentioned what had happened that night. I often wonder why she didn't tell her mother, but I never asked. I assumed she knew she hadn't asked her mother if she could go out with her sister and me, and she feared she would get in trouble. Although she was underage, she looked mature enough to go to the Red Rose Club. I don't remember if she was punished for going out with me that night, but I remember her mother did not take what happened to me lightly. Just like my father, Dorothy's mother wanted to punish Robert.

After my father told Dorothy's mother what happened, she was so upset and wanted to hear what Dorothy had to say. Dorothy was outside in the backyard. Immediately, her mother went to the back door and asked Dorothy to come inside the house because she wanted to talk to her. Dorothy had this surprised look on her face when she greeted my father and me. After her mother told her about the rape, she asked why Dorothy didn't tell her. Dorothy stood there like it was no big deal. She seemed to be bothered that I was there telling her mother.

When Dorothy's mother asked why she didn't want to testify, she said, "She shouldn't have done it." I could not speak! I didn't want to believe she said those awful words. I opened my mouth, but no words came out. I just stood there and cried. My father and Dorothy's mother tried to console me. How dare Dorothy have no empathy and say it was my fault? Her testimony was my only chance! She had to testify so that Robert could be punished for his violent behavior and how it affected both of us that awful night.

Dorothy turned her back on me when I needed her the most. She would not cooperate with her mother or my father's decision to report Robert to the law. She refused to be a witness and showed no empathy.

It became apparent that Dorothy had taken that night's crime less seriously than I had. She left me with a burden that was heavy and difficult to carry alone. We were both witnesses to what happened that night. Robert raped me, and it would have made no sense for me to have talked to my parents about it if the sex had been consensual. I was not having sex with anyone. I wasn't dating and had no boyfriend.

My father left Dorothy's house, hoping that once we left, her mother could convince her to change her mind and testify. He was wrong. Dorothy's refusal was her definitive answer. Without her testimony, my parents felt there wasn't a case. They believed she wouldn't talk, even if she received a subpoena. I've never understood why Dorothy didn't want to testify. I wonder if her failure to testify influenced our other cousins' opinions on my father's side of the family.

I do not know how the news spread about that night. Somehow, it had gotten into the ears of some of my cousins. There was a lot of gossiping going on, and mostly all my cousins said, "She shouldn't have done it." I couldn't believe they had ignored the fact that Robert forced me at gunpoint to do something I was unwilling to do. It was overwhelming that they believed it was my fault. Those horrible words Dorothy said, "She shouldn't have done it!" kept echoing in my head. I'd had no doubt in my mind she would be there for me. Boy, was I wrong!

This is why so many survivors can relate to Dr. Ford's story. They are afraid society will blame them for a crime they could not control.

My parents' hands were tied. My father couldn't afford a lawyer. We didn't understand that legal representation would have been helpful to direct my father to make the best decisions in the matter. The only person I knew who could help me was the one person my mother did not want me to tell—my older brother David. My parents knew if David got involved, he would have retaliated with bodily harm if he were still living with us. Being the oldest, he had gotten married about four years prior and had moved away to another town. I often wanted to go against my promise to my mother and tell my brother what happened. He'd always been there for me, especially when kids bullied me in the community or at school. He was my protector. I will always regret that I didn't get a chance to tell him about that horrible night before he died in 2002.

I remember the moment I learned of his passing vividly. I nearly fainted when my cousin Florence came to my mother's house and told us my brother had been killed. He was driving his favorite burgundy truck on the way to my mother's house when a tree his neighbor was cutting down in his front yard killed him. The neighbor couldn't control the tree falling onto my brother's truck, and it killed him instantly.

Dorothy and I didn't talk about that night again. I suppressed the memory of the rape. It was as if it had never happened. Our relationship, however, ended the day her mother and my father confronted her. My parents would have forbidden me to go out with them again anyway.

I am sure Robert continued taking advantage of and attacking other women. When I learned he bragged about how he took advantage of women to have sex with him, I probably was one of those women he bragged about. I wondered if the others were threatened by his gun. More so, I wondered if they ever told anyone. For years, I struggled with intense anger. I wanted Robert punished.

That he faced no consequences meant Robert had won! I blamed myself and began to believe it was my fault. I convinced myself that it would never have happened if I had not gone out that night. For a long time, I felt empty; I was withdrawn and depressed. I didn't trust anyone anymore. I didn't have any close friends or cousins I wanted to be around. When I went out, it was only with my family. I wasn't working at the time, so I just sat in the house preparing to go to Pitt Community College in the fall.

Once I was in school, doing homework and meeting new friends helped with the depression. I'd thought nothing like that would happen to me. I had no self-worth. Other than my family, I didn't associate with anyone for a while. I was too ashamed. I just wanted that night to go away. My mind went deep into suppressing the memory so I wouldn't have to deal with it. After that, when I heard of someone that had been sexually assaulted or saw it happen as part of a TV show, I tried to tune out that it also had happened to me. I wanted to move on. Unfortunately, that was easier said than done. The flashbacks of the pain, fear, and shame surrounding sexual trauma continue to haunt me still.

To cope, I buried everything about that night beyond the level of consciousness. Forgetting was how I survived. I buried that night so deep in my mind that I can't even bring myself to remember the type of car we were in. Honestly, I have no recollection of what I was wearing. I'm almost sure I had on a dress because back then I didn't wear pants. I know I never wore those clothes again.

There were two things I never denied in my mind: the sight of the gun and the monster's face. Most victims hardly remember the material things, but the physical details haunt you forever.

I'm a Survivor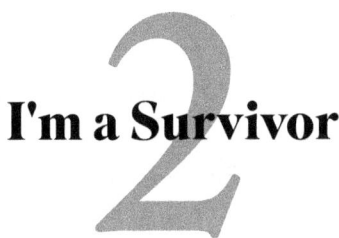

Like most survivors, I believed it was in my best interest to suppress the rape. I refused to discuss that night and pretended that it never happened. I didn't realize that the suppression of sexual assault can lead to many unresolved psychological issues. The first experience I had with the invisible monster was while riding in my father's first car he had purchased approximately three months after the rape.

The moment I sat down in the front seat of the dark blue Buick, I admired the light-colored interior, which made the car look brand new. I was as happy as my father that day because he no longer depended on the few people in the community who had cars to take us places.

We weren't rich, and my father couldn't afford a car until I turned eighteen. Before we had a car, we walked a mile to the main highway to hitchhike or take the Trailways bus when we wanted to shop in Greenville. Hitchhiking was a widespread practice in rural areas back then, and it was safer than it is today.

My father didn't ride the Trailways bus that much. He couldn't afford it. The bus came by twice a day, going to and from Greenville. However, it was during the Jim Crow era when Blacks had to sit in the back of the bus while whites sat in the front. In 1955, Rosa Parks' refusal initiated change, culminating in the Supreme Court's 1956 decision to end segregation in public transportation.

My father drove at a snail's pace, and I noticed several men working on the highway. I really can't explain why, but as my father drove closer, and I looked into the faces of those men, I flashed back to the night Robert raped me. I trembled in fear, feeling as if I were being smothered. I had heart palpitations too—my heart skipped beats and sped up, turning somersaults. I looked at my father, realizing that he didn't notice my reaction because he didn't say anything. I was too afraid to tell him what I felt: I just wanted my father to enjoy driving his new car. But I was losing my mind. It was like a monster attacking me. It felt like someone grabbed my neck, choked me, and I couldn't defend myself.

I had no clue what it was. It happened so quickly. Never would I imagine that this was the beginning of a nightmare I would struggle with for the rest of my life. I wanted to escape. I kept taking long, deep breaths, trying to relax. The entire experience lasted only a few minutes, but it felt like it would never end.

I did not know what was happening. I had an overwhelming feeling that something was wrong with me. No one in their right mind would experience those feelings. I had no clue what to do, and my father probably would not have known what to do either. I decided not to tell anyone that I was going crazy. Besides, I thought it would never happen again. So, I kept it a secret.

During that time, when someone had a strange reaction that wasn't physical, we didn't go to a doctor. My family and some members of the church would pray with you or just thought you were crazy. For a long time, I regretted I didn't tell anyone about that experience.

I remember my cousin, who lived about six miles from me, experiencing terrifying reactions. He would run and scream for no reason. No one knew what to do. They didn't take him to a doctor because they knew it wasn't physical. Also, we didn't go to the doctor for most things because we couldn't afford it. Most people I knew had never even considered going to a psychiatrist either. We just prayed. I said a prayer and kept that experience a secret because most people with mental problems then were often regarded as having a shameful character flaw.

After that, whenever I was stressed, frightened, or triggered by anything reminding me of that night, I experienced those terrifying feelings. They lasted for only a few seconds. I prayed that the feeling would go away for good.

I had many fears when I was a child, but they didn't have lasting repercussions. When I worked in the fields and saw a snake, I would almost die of fear. During a thunderstorm, my siblings and I would migrate to one room, sit in the dark, and remain silent until the storm was over. If I knew of someone who died in the neighborhood, I had difficulty sleeping because I imagined encountering a ghost.

I still struggle today with the fear of snakes and destructive storms, especially if there's a warning of a tornado or hurricane nearby. I act the same way I did when I was a child, huddling in a room until it's over. I also suffered from the fear of being bullied and social anxiety. I didn't particularly appreciate going to high school until my junior year because my cousin Ana and her friends bullied me. What I regret is that I didn't fight back. Although she was only a little bigger than me, I was too afraid to stand up for myself. My cousin was aggressive. She had a big mouth. Every day she had a confrontation with some of the kids at school. Most kids feared her power. On the first day of high school, when the girls from Simpson Elementary School exited the bus, we went to the bathroom to freshen up. Ana and her friends busted inside the bathroom, harassing us, and threatening to fight us. We just ignored their threats, and Ana and her friends finally left the bathroom.

Simpson Elementary School was the only Black school located in Simpson. Kids in the surrounding area near Simpson rode the bus. Everyone who lived in Simpson could walk to school. I lived beside the school. It took me less than two minutes to walk across the yard onto the school grounds. My father often talked about how his generation could not go to high school after they finished the eighth grade because it was too far away. White kids rode to school on the bus while Black people had to walk. Unlike my father, when I finished Simpson Elementary School, the county had provided bus transportation to the high school in Grimesland. The kids who lived in Simpson would board the bus at Simpson Elementary School to go to high school. The high school bus driver was one of my classmates that lived about three miles from Simpson. Unlike today, back then, student bus drivers were the norm. The high school's name changed when I was in the eleventh grade.

The day I graduated from Simpson Elementary School was a big deal for me. I was so excited that I was going to high school until my cousin took the joy of it away from me. Why she wanted to pick a fight with the Simpson girls that day in the bathroom I never understood. I was so afraid and stood there trembling in my stall. I wanted to run, but there was no way to escape, so I just prayed, "Lord, please don't let my cousin hit me. I am too afraid to fight this girl."

One of the Simpson girls, Len, was very assertive. She stood up to the bullying. I stayed close to her because I knew she would defend me and the other girls. After that, my cousin and her friends bullied us during lunch.

I thought the bullying would stop when our Aunt Corene intervened and told Ana that she should be ashamed of bullying me. But that didn't stop her. It didn't matter that my father was her uncle either. She refused to tell our classmates that she and I were cousins. Every day, I prayed that the bullying would stop, but it continued until she dropped out of school in the eleventh grade. Thank God he answered by prayers.

The environment changed miraculously. It was smooth sailing until I graduated. My cousin never knew how much her aggressive behavior influenced my life. Unfortunately, I never talked to her about it. So many times, at our family reunion, I wanted to talk to her about her bullying. However, I decided to let bygones be bygones. Then, one day when we were planning our family reunion, she had an attitude because she couldn't park her car in my yard. She would not be in control this time! I stood up to her, spoke in a not-so-pleasant tone, and explained why she couldn't park in the yard. I realized I was no longer afraid of her.

My older brother, David, and older sister, Bell, often fought my battles for me as a child. I was an introvert and very shy. Growing up, I was always afraid because of my size: I was the smallest of all my siblings. This low self-esteem led me to believe I was a nobody. I knew in my heart that everyone in my family loved me. But the teasing made me depressed. This had a significant effect on my struggle with social anxiety. I felt like I didn't fit in around my peers and grew tired of being teased about my size. Sometimes the teasing would be friendly, sometimes neutral, and sometimes harmful. That was a big issue for me.

When we were changing classes, two of the students in a higher grade noticed I was wearing silk stockings. One girl said to her friend, "Look at Mary Parker wearing silk stockings with those skinny legs." The other girl laughed. I said nothing and started walking fast to get away from them. They continued to laugh until I went into the classroom. I was so embarrassed and too afraid to defend myself. My eyes welled with tears as I tried to hold them back. After that incident, I vowed I would never wear silk stockings to school again, even though most girls in high school wore them. It wasn't until the day I graduated that I gathered enough courage to wear silk stockings again. I had on a long gown, and no one could see my skinny legs. I was seventeen and wanted to be like everyone else my age, but I often wondered if people were making fun of me behind my back.

I had two best friends I felt comfortable being around. We communicated with each other only at school because we had no phones and didn't live near each other. Most people in my community couldn't afford a phone or a television. We had radios. I was a junior in high school when my parents bought their first black-and-white TV in the late '60s. We got a phone after I had graduated from high school. I continue to communicate with one of these two friends. The other friend, sadly, passed away several years ago.

I was too shy to date in high school. When a guy wanted to take me on a date, I would always say, "No, I'm not going out with you." One day, my teacher needed a list of students who were attending the prom. One of the well-to-do guys in my class blurted out that he wanted to take me. It was like a bomb going off in the classroom. Everyone in the class laughed. I sat there wanting to die. I thought, *Why me?* Most likely, I would not have accepted the invitation. Going to the prom with him would have been awkward, as we'd never talked, but I'll never know because he never asked. I assumed he was too embarrassed because of our classmates' reactions. I didn't have a date for my junior and senior year proms, but I had a great time at both proms. I wore the same pink dress both years because my mother could not afford to buy me two new dresses. The first time I wore the dress, most of the girls at the prom had on that same dress, but in different colors. It appeared everyone had purchased their dress from the same store. Most people shopped at the same stores because we didn't have that many clothing stores in Greenville. When everyone started dancing, the different colors of dresses looked like a rainbow had appeared in the center of the floor.

I will never forget the day I had a serious conversation with my sister about how I felt about myself. I was in my late twenties and had just sat down to eat dinner. When I told her how I felt, she disagreed with me. She said, "Mary, you shouldn't feel like you are not worthy. Don't let that define who you are. You are somebody. We are God's children." Those were powerful words I needed to hear.

My oldest sister has always been a religious person. She received salvation at an early age and sang in the choir, taught Sunday school, and was a "mother" of the church. She has always been the family leader among the siblings, telling us what to do or not to do. No matter what, we would listen to her advice. I will also never forget the words my late husband used to say to me: "You know, I like skinny women." Those words still resonate with me today because when someone calls me skinny, I'll say to them, "My late husband liked skinny women. I don't worry about anyone else." What my sister and late husband said encouraged me to build steps toward improving my self-esteem.

Life Goes On

I got my first real job working in a factory at the company Hamilton Beach in Washington, North Carolina, working the night shift from 3:00 p.m. to 11:00 p.m. I thought the job was going to be a long-term job. Then one night out of the blue, my boss said, "If you can't work overtime, I no longer need you to work here." It didn't matter to him; I had to get a ride to work with the lady that lived near me. I didn't drive, nor did I have a car. The lady and I worked on the same floor, but we did different things. I couldn't expect her to wait until my shift ended. I didn't like that job anyway. Every night when I went home after work, my hands would be wrinkled from the cleaning fluid I used to clean the equipment.

I met Elmo during this same period. It took me two years after I'd been raped to go on my first date. I wasn't sure if I could trust a man. Elmo and his family were well known when his family moved to Simpson. He and his four brothers were very popular with the girls in the surrounding area. All of them were good-looking—that drew the girls to them. For a million years, I never thought I would date one of the brothers. When Elmo wanted a date with me, I didn't give him an answer right away. Most people had described Elmo as a womanizer, and I had difficulty motivating myself to be social after a busy and stressful night at work.

I went to the corner store one day to buy some snaps, and Elmo was standing outside. As I was leaving the store, he was flirting with me about my appearance. Finally, he got the nerve to ask me for a date. I said no. I wasn't sure if I could trust him. About three months later, surprisingly, I accepted his invitation to go on a date. He was good-looking and seemed like a nice person. But I was hesitant because he was three years older than me and likely more experienced as well. We went to a club on our first date; it didn't go so well.

We double-dated with his brother and my cousin Lenette. Elmo didn't have a car. I was very uncomfortable sitting in the back seat with him. When Elmo touched me, I pushed him away, as it triggered a flashback to the night Robert assaulted me. I know it's natural to be nervous on the first date, but all I could think about was that night I was raped. The only time I felt comfortable and safe was when we went inside the club. I could relax when I saw people there. The Hardy Club had just opened near Simpson, and most of the people from my town hung out there. I never went to the Red Rose Club again. But it had fallen out of favor anyway. It wasn't popular anymore. Almost everyone was going to the Hardy Club. It was closer to Simpson.

When Elmo asked me to dance with him, I said no. I was too nervous. I never had a fast dance with a guy before. And I didn't know how good a dancer he was. After he had asked me several times, I gained enough nerve to slow dance with him. I was afraid he could dance better than me. I had never seemed him dance, and I didn't dance publicly.

Now, at home was a different story; I danced all the time. Sometimes the music would be so loud, my parents would say, "Girl, turn that music down so I can hear the TV!" When the date ended, I agreed to go out with Elmo again when he asked if he could take me out the next weekend. I never felt comfortable being with Elmo. When we went out, we mostly double-dated with his brother and his brother's girlfriend. I don't think I gave myself enough time to feel connected to someone I could trust.

When my relationship with Elmo was falling apart, I questioned whether I should fix it or move on with my life. Besides my nervousness, his ex-girlfriend was constantly interfering with our relationship. He told me it was over between them and that he'd told her to stop calling and sending him letters. I believe he was trying to get away from her, but I couldn't deal with another woman. It was disrespectful, and that made me feel insecure. I was not happy.

. . .

One day, my sister, Bell, said to me, "Mary, I want you to come to live with me in New Jersey." She assured me I would get a good job, and things would be better than living in the South. My sister had landed a great job working in an office. She hoped I would get a job working with her. I had to make a conscious decision: go live with my sister or fix my relationship with my boyfriend.

I knew there were pros and cons no matter where I lived. I wasn't sure if I could adapt to living in the North. When my father and I had visited my sister for Easter that year in Newark, New Jersey, I didn't like the city—it was too crowded and had a high crime rate. I'd never seen such tall buildings before and so many people in all my life. Night and day, I heard sirens from ambulances and fire trucks constantly racing up and down the streets. When my sister took me and my father shopping at the mall, I was scared to ride the escalator—I had never seen one before. It took my father and me a while to gather the courage to put our feet on the first step while it was moving. And it had snowed more than six inches the night before my father and I took the bus back to North Carolina. I had never seen that much snow. My father and I didn't have the right clothing to be prepared for that type of weather. I couldn't get back home fast enough. I swore I would never go back to New Jersey. But my sister didn't stop until she convinced me to move to join her. She convinced me when she said, "I know you could get a better job in the north. We could work together and share an apartment." I really had nothing to lose. If things didn't work out, I could always go back home.

I knew going up north would be much better for me. It would be easier to get a job working in an office like my sister. In the '60s, Black people were excluded from getting higher-paying jobs in the South. So, I resigned from working at the Hourglass Cleaner as a presser. I appreciated my cousin Ruby for helping me get a job there after Hamilton Beach let me go, but I wanted something better. Ruby wanted a better job as well. She resigned several months before me and moved to New Jersey to live with her aunt. I had finished high school and completed one year of secretary school at Pitt Technical Institute, and I wanted to work in an office.

A New Start

It was September 1970 when I left North Carolina and moved to New Jersey. It was the same night I broke up with my boyfriend. I called Elmo to come to my house that night several hours before I planned to board the bus. He did not know I was breaking up with him. I knew if I told him my plan, he would have talked me out of it. Whenever I tried to break up with him, he would always have such a way with words to change my mind. He didn't believe I was leaving until he saw my suitcase packed. It was the hardest thing I had to do, but we both knew we were not compatible to make a long-term relationship work. He had no ambition, and it had started to bother me.

    I knew it was only a matter of time before my relationship with him would end, because I could no longer deal with his ex. She didn't want to let him go when we started dating. I remember one night we went on a date at our favorite club. She was there and had a confrontation with him in front of everyone. That was the last straw for me. He couldn't control her actions, and I had no interest in fighting over a man. I was sure my decision was best for both of us. Going to New Jersey was the only way for me to fulfill my potential.

    September was a perfect time for me to move to New Jersey because it was when my aunt and uncle went to visit their children for Labor Day weekend. Taking a bus to travel to a big city on my own would have scared me. On the bus ride, I sat beside my aunt Lue. When I closed my eyes to relax and enjoy the ride, all I could think about was how sad my ex had looked when I kissed him goodbye. But I had made up my mind, and there was no turning back. I had to do what I had to do. I tried focusing on living in the moment and not dwelling on the past or being too anxious about the future. After all, relocating to a big city was different from life in my hometown. Living in a big city was my first step to achieving my goal. My dream of becoming a secretary in the South was slim. Just about everyone from my generation moved up north once they finished high school. This was during the great migration. And the only way to escape segregation in the South was to migrate to the North for a better standard of living, the way my sister had done. Within days after she moved to New Jersey, she'd landed an excellent job, and I was expecting to do the same.

For a while, my sister and I shared an apartment with our cousin Marion. She lived in a three-story apartment building. One thing I had to get used to was always being aware of my surroundings. The entrance door to the apartment building always had to be locked. I made sure whenever I went out that I held my purse tightly and close to my body, whether on a bus, train, or walking down the street. Where I came from, most people in the South did not have to worry about keeping their doors or windows locked. And I never heard of anyone snatching someone's purse. But a lot has changed since then.

Immediately, I applied for a job at my sister's workplace, but there were no available positions. Everywhere I went, there were no openings. It was a challenge. I applied to do secretarial work, but I had no experience. Three months had passed when I said to my sister, "If I don't find something soon, I'm going back home." I had gotten tired and frustrated. Marion said I should apply to New Jersey Bell. It was my last hope of getting a job.

When I walked toward the tall white New Jersey Bell building to apply for a job, I couldn't help but notice that I had never seen a building that tall before. I was so nervous going around the revolving door, I almost went around again! Thank God the receptionist area was on the first floor—it was a significant relief knowing that I did not have to go on the elevator to another floor. I immediately developed a fear of heights and worried that I might pass out if I had to ride in the elevator alone to a higher level. Back home, we didn't have escalators or high-rise buildings. I was anxious about getting a job. I did not need that added stress.

When I saw all those people filling out applications in the reception area of the phone company, I had no confidence I would get a job. But I filled out an application anyway and took the two-hour-long written test. I was thankful the test was multiple choice and there was no typing test. While waiting to be interviewed, I observed people who were not hired leaving the interviewer's office. Some of them said, "That test was hard; I knew I wasn't going to pass." I was not expecting to be hired either. I was the last person to be interviewed that day. The first thing the lady asked me was what type of position I was applying for. I had deliberately omitted that section on the application. It didn't matter what position they would offer me. I said, "I just want a job doing anything."

The lady chuckled. She said, "We don't hire for just anything. You have to be specific." I responded, "I would like to do clerical work." I remember that was one position my sister said I should apply for. I did not have any secretarial experience, and I did not want to hear the same song that there were no openings. My hand raised to God, and I thanked Him because the lady said I'd passed the test, and she offered me a job to work at another location.

As soon as I got the job offer at New Jersey Bell, I was offered a job back home. I had applied for a job at Kmart and Burroughs Wellcome. They had relocated to Greenville a couple of months before I went to New Jersey. My mother wasn't sure who had called me for a job. She just said, "One of those places you applied for a job called you. They want you to start working right away." I would have accepted the job offer if I had not already moved. I don't know if that was a blessing or a curse, because once I started working at New Jersey Bell, my life became a living nightmare.

The first day I went to work, I was jittery. I arrived about half an hour early, walking a block from the bus stop to a tall brick building on Washington Street. The building was not as tall as the main office. I took the elevator to the sixth floor, where I was assigned to work. Upon entering the elevator, I was relieved that I was not alone, and I could watch how the other people pushed the button for different floors. I didn't want anyone thinking I didn't know how to ride in it. The elevators in the department stores, which I rode on back home, only went to the second or third floor, and people had to operate it manually.

Right away, I liked the head boss, Rob. He was much nicer than his boss. He had patience with me and made sure I understood the job. Everyone in the office had to be trained when the job changed their rules on how to answer the phone more professionally. They gave us other clerical duties as well. Rob felt I was the most qualified person to train. Joann, the supervisor, had an attitiude problem. I could work with her, but I didn't like how she ran the office. When you asked for help, her attitude was snappy. She was moody and difficult to work with. She micromanaged every task she assigned you to do, and it negatively affected the employees' morale.

It was a challenge working with about thirty men and women in one office. It took me some time to understand the different nationalities of people and their cultures. It was the first time that I'd seen people from Central America, Africa, Cuba, Mexico, and other places worldwide. Where I was from, the only people I encountered were black and white people from the South. I liked how everyone in the office called me by my correct name, Mary Sue. The supervisor called me by my first and middle names because there was another person in the office named Mary. People down south called me Mary Lee. That's what my father named me. But the nurse at the hospital where I was born put Mary Sue on my record. My father didn't change it, so that's what I go by.

Most of the calls I received were common problems with either home or business phones. The northern accent was way more diverse than the southern accent. Right away, the customers recognized my thick southern dialect. In the beginning, I had a problem communicating with them. One day, an angry customer called for service, and when I asked him, "What's the trouble?" he kept repeating, "Did you say color?" That upset me, but I could not retaliate. It didn't matter to the phone company if the customers were friendly or angry. We had to abide by their vision statement, "Being good is not good enough." When I realized the customer was not understanding what I was saying, I just spelled t-r-o-u-b-l-e.

I was making good money. It was more than I made in the South. I was looking forward to a fantastic future. I'd thought the fear of the invisible monster would go away when I moved and was far away from where the attack had happened. I was wrong.

I experienced the recurring invisible monster unexpectedly shortly after I started working at New Jersey Bell. When I got off work after a very stressful day, my coworker Mattie and I had gotten on the bus to go home, and it was full of people. We were packed in like sardines. People were standing in the aisle. My coworker and I were lucky to get a seat in the back. That's when it hit: I couldn't breathe. My body was out of control. It felt weird and there was nothing I could do about it. Suddenly, I was experiencing dizziness, blurry vision, and my heart was beating fast. It was far more terrifying than the first one I encountered. I was so afraid; I thought I was going to die. The more people there were around me, the harder it was for me to breathe. Mattie had no clue what I was experiencing. I dared not tell her, just like I didn't tell my father when I rode in his car. I did not want her or anyone thinking I was losing my mind. I had the same feeling of wanting to escape, like that night I was raped.

As the weird feeling escalated, my coworker talked to me, but I wasn't listening. I couldn't tell you what she said to me. I didn't say anything to her, and I just wanted to scream. My anxiety was going through the roof. The ride to my stop felt like forever. Once I got off the bus, I composed myself. I just wanted to breathe in some fresh air. I prayed, "Lord, why is this invisible monster following me around? Please let it stop."

Every afternoon when I got on the bus heading home, I had an intense fear of dealing with the invisible monster. I don't know if it happened because I expected one because I'd had a stressful day, or because I was riding on a crowded bus. I dreaded going home after work. It was like living with an invisible monster on my back that I could not get rid of. I had no clue what to do. I was too afraid to tell anyone, even my sister. It was difficult for me to be myself around people.

I kept thinking things were going to get better. I was hoping the nightmare would go away. When the working conditions of my job changed, that created stress. I was under a tremendous amount of pressure. I took lots of calls from customers with telephone problems. The phone rang all day long. I was required to take a minimum of one hundred phone calls per day.

Some days, they assigned me to work on the Teletype machine that was in a small office. It was less stressful because I worked alone, and it was quiet with no interruptions. I didn't have to worry about the supervisors breathing down my neck. We had to cross every *t* and dot every *i*. Thank God I was not required to answer phone calls.

Moving Forward

John and I were friends before we moved to New Jersey. The day I met him was like a breath of fresh air. It felt like we'd known each other for years. Right away, he brought sunshine into my life on my cloudy days. With his funny jokes and talking a mile a minute, I felt comfortable opening up to him. He said things to make me feel good about myself. I was depressed for so long after the rape. Laughing and talking with John made me feel alive again. He was different and seemed more excited than most people I had been around. John was staying with his cousin Bill to attend Pitt Technical Institute, where I went. (It later became Pitt Community College.) I rode to PCC with Bill every day, along with his cousin John and my friend Carolyn. Because of my friendship with John and the confidence I'd built from school, I was effectively interacting with people outside my family.

Going to school and meeting people, I had new friends, and sometimes we studied together. Homework kept me occupied every day. I could concentrate on other things other than that dreadful night. When I started school, my father had installed his first telephone. I was so excited. Every day after I finished my homework, I called my friends from school. Sometimes we would talk until bedtime.

At lunchtime, John was fun to be around. He would come and sit with me and the other students. He would tell these hilarious jokes that cracked you up. His jokes were so silly, I would laugh so hard until tears ran down my face.

All the black students sat together in the lunchroom. One day, John and I were sitting in the lunchroom when some of the black students rushed to the snack machine to get free snacks because someone had discovered the machine was broken. The white students sat there looking at the black students getting free snacks until the machine was almost empty. A white student reported the incident to the school. We were so afraid we had gotten ourselves into serious trouble. Luckily, the school was more concerned about getting the machine repaired.

When PCC had dances, John, Bill, Carolyn, and I always went to the dances together. We enjoyed listening to the band play our favorite songs, dancing, laughing, and talking with the students. The dances only cost one dollar at the door, but sometimes Carolyn paid for me when I didn't have the money. I often told her that is something I will be grateful for until the day I die. She still maintains that same spirit of helping others even now.

I remember how hard it was for John to say goodbye when he came by my house before he left for Vietnam. We kept in touch for two years. I contacted John when I moved to New Jersey, knowing he had moved to New Brunswick, New Jersey, only forty-five minutes from where I lived. Our platonic relationship ended when we both lived in New Jersey, and we began to date. It was now a romantic relationship. I didn't see it coming until after our first kiss, while we were on our first date. Every weekend, John would come to see me. He didn't know his surroundings in Newark that well, so we didn't go to many places. Sometimes, I would take the train to visit him.

I had no doubt that my relationship with John was heading in the right direction. One time, I'd taken the train down to see him and felt like I could deal with that invisible monster on the train because it was a short ride; I could breathe my way through it. Fortunately, the train was less crowded than the bus. John was staying with his father and stepmother until he found his own place, and I thought the visit went well. His grandfather was visiting from down south that weekend. John took us shopping and sightseeing.

My conversation with John turned sour abruptly as he drove me home. Suddenly, his tone of voice changed. He was beside himself. For almost a year we had been dating, I had not seen this sudden change of attitude. It was like he changed from a human man into a monster. When he raised his voice at me, I was shocked. His tone was harsh and aggressive.

He was criticizing everything about me. The way I acted. The way I looked. He didn't like my thick southern accent. I was not "sophisticated" enough for him. John's negative judgment made me so uncomfortable—I just wanted to get away from him. His attitude and mannerisms were not the same as the person I'd become friends with at PCC.

Now that I thought about it, we weren't laughing and joking the way we had been at school. I wondered if he had PTSD after being in Vietnam. His behavior triggered a flashback to that night I was raped. His tone of voiced scared me, and I didn't know if he was going to rape me or if he was just verbally abusive. I was experiencing anxiety and suddenly became so anxious that I felt like I couldn't breathe. I was faint and dizzy. I wanted John to stop the car so that I could escape that horrible feeling. But I knew it was impossible. While he was talking, I ignored him. My focus was on what was happening to me. I just prayed to the Lord to please help me. That forty-five-minute ride felt like forever.

When we reached Newark, I didn't know my way around that well. I had not been living there long enough to know some of the street names. I only knew the street that would take me to my apartment. John didn't know his way around either. Before he'd gotten the car, he took the train and a taxi to visit me. As we were approaching Broad Street, I told him to make a right turn. I don't know if he understood what I said because he ended up on Broadway Street instead. It was a one-way street, and we were going in the opposite direction. When John realized he had made a wrong turn, he was afraid he was going to collide with someone. He sped up the car to get off the one-way street as fast as he could. He clenched his jaw, and I saw intense anger in his eyes. He was screaming when he said, "You don't know how to get to your apartment?" And before I could respond, he slapped me so hard across my face that I saw stars. This astonished me as much as it shocked me. I cried. I had never seen him like that before. It wasn't my fault he made the wrong turn.

He kept going around in a circle, trying to find Broad Street. I felt some relief when he finally reached the right street. I dared not say a word. I just thought, *When I get out of this car, I will never talk to you again.*

I was just a naïve southern girl. I spent most of my life letting people walk all over me. John was no exception. When John didn't apologize for slapping me, that was the end of the rope. Even though I was too afraid to fight back, I felt it was best to end the relationship. After that incident, I didn't go out with him again. I talked to his stepmother and told her what John had done which upset him.

He called to confront me about the conversation, but it went nowhere. At that point, I realized his lousy attitude was something I couldn't deal with. Ultimately, we both reached the agreement that we weren't meant for each other.

My First Apartment

One day at work, my friend Mattie overheard me saying something about looking for an apartment. Mattie didn't say anything right then, but on the way to the bus stop that afternoon, she told me she had a vacant apartment upstairs in her two-family house. She wanted to know if my sister and I were interested, and if so, we could come by to view the apartment.

The neighborhood was nice, and I was somewhat familiar with the area, which was several blocks from where I lived. My sister and I were having a hard time finding a place we liked. Right away, we went to see the apartment. When Mattie took us upstairs to see the three-room apartment, my first thought was that it was not big enough. I had reservations about living in an apartment with ceilings that were too low and shaped like an attic. I should have known it would be a big problem, but I didn't tell my sister how I felt about the place. It was more space than at my cousin's. My sister was enthusiastic, so I agreed to rent the apartment.

Once we placed our furniture in the apartment, it was much smaller than I initially thought. I had a problem sitting in the living room with the two doors closed beside my sister's bedroom and the kitchen. I felt like I was suffocating in the dark. The small window facing the north side of the apartment didn't bring enough light into the living room. It was like being in a cave, and that was a big problem for me. After we moved into the apartment, we learned from Mattie that she had turned the second floor into an upstairs apartment. It was initially a one-family house.

Soon after we moved, that unexpected feeling attacked me. It appeared out of nowhere one night. Suddenly, the room was spinning, and I felt like I was suffocating. I was alone, afraid, and thought I was going to die. My sister had gone down south on vacation, and I didn't know what to do. I raced downstairs to Mattie's apartment and told her I wasn't feeling well. I was too ashamed to tell her how I felt. I just said, "I'm sick." Mattie stopped what she was doing and rushed to the phone to call a taxi to take me to the hospital. By the way she looked at me, I could tell she was scared. I was feeling dizzy and light-headed. She thought I was going to faint.

As I was sitting in the examination room at the hospital waiting on the doctor, I contemplated what to tell him. I didn't know how to explain my problem. I thought I was losing my mind. My body was out of control. I felt out of touch with reality, and I dared not tell him that. I'm sure he would have labeled me as crazy. That was a half-truth. For years I had a sinus problem, but not to the extent that I had to see a doctor. When I would get stuffy, I used a Vicks inhaler to help me breathe. I didn't learn until later that these strange feelings could also affect your nose and cause different nasal symptoms. I hoped my sinuses were the only issue and that my problem would resolve itself. After he examined me, he said I was having a problem with low blood pressure. And there was nothing wrong with my sinuses. I don't remember how the doctor discovered I had low blood pressure. I just took the medication he prescribed, but often wondered if that medication was what I needed. After that attack, I avoided sitting in the living room with the door next to the kitchen closed.

The breathing problems were becoming more and more intense. I worried it would interfere with my daily life. It was a challenge keeping my condition a secret from my family and other people. My avoidance behaviors were preventing me from living life to the fullest. I feared riding the bus, car, and train. Dating was nerve-racking, as I worried about the invisible monster showing up and interfering while on a date. I did my best to avoid having to explain what I was experiencing. When I went on a date, I was so uncomfortable. After I ended my relationship with John, I didn't date for a while. I didn't go anywhere. I often wonder if my life would have been better had I not suppressed the sexual attack.

7

A New Love: Jackson

Jackson was the type of guy any girl wouldn't mind dating. He drove an expensive white Cadillac. He was of medium build, light complexion, and handsome.

When Jackson came into the office to pick up his work assignments, he would walk to my desk before leaving and start a conversation. When I saw him coming toward where I was sitting, he would stare at me with those big, beautiful eyes and smile. I felt attracted to him. He was someone who was interesting and listened to the things you had to say. I believe he would have been even more attractive if he didn't have a long beard. He didn't want to shave it off, so I didn't let that interfere with our relationship when we started dating.

Jackson was the only person I communicated with regularly. When I first started working at the phone company, I was friends with some women in the office. We went out on some social occasions. But I soon realized they mostly wanted to drink and go to bars, and I didn't drink, so I felt out of place. Everyone in the office drank alcohol except for me. With my Christian upbringing, I felt drinking alcohol and smoking were sins, so I disconnected from the women. I didn't trust most of them anyway. Although I got along well with them, I didn't like that they would say one thing to your face and something else behind your back. There were a lot of catty women's issues going on in the office. My friendship with the men differed greatly from my friendship with the women. Most of the men seemed to be down-to-earth.

Jackson and I both worked in the same building at the phone company, but on different floors. Jackson had been working for AT&T for many years before I started at New Jersey Bell. A lot of times, when I called Jackson about a problem with a phone number, we wouldn't be talking about work. We talked about other things. Eventually, he asked me out.

At the beginning of our relationship, Jackson showed love and respect toward me. He made me feel comfortable. I could relax around him. He was a gentleman and made sure I was safe. He was my protector. Our relationship was strictly platonic; I didn't have to worry about him wanting sex or forcing himself on me. I often wondered whether he was gay or straight. I learned later he was straight when he dated a friend I knew, and they had a baby. It didn't bother me not to have sex because I wasn't in any rush. I was cool with it.

After the rape, I avoided sex because I didn't want to experience the intense fear that something dreadful would happen to me. When he came by to see me at Mattie's house, where I was living, I didn't dare tell him I couldn't sit in the living room with the door closed. We talked, joked, and watched TV. I didn't have to worry about privacy because my sister went to bed early most of the time.

Jackson asked me to go with him to Atlantic City one Saturday to visit his friend who owned a bar and restaurant. Immediately, fear prompted me to say no. I had a flashback to the time I had that overwhelming feeling of my body losing control riding in the car with John. Although I was fearful, I decided not to let fear deter me. I wanted to go because I'd heard how people liked the beach and walking on the boardwalk. I wanted to see what Atlantic City looked like. Going to the beach was something I didn't do much in North Carolina. I had been to a beach only once. The closest beach for Black people was about twenty miles away from where I grew up. I needed a weekend getaway. I pushed myself to accept the invitation.

We had been riding on the parkway for almost an hour when I started gasping for air, and it was hard for me to stop fidgeting in my seat. I was losing control. Occasionally, Jackson would look at me sitting on the passenger side, taking deep breaths and placing my hand on my heart. At first, he didn't say anything. As we continued to ride, however, I became more anxious. Finally, he asked, "Are you okay?" I repeated the same sad story I said to everyone who noticed when I did this. "I'm having a problem with my sinuses."

Jackson turned the vent on high when I said I needed some air and water. I knew that would not solve the problem, but I didn't tell him to turn it off. It was hard for me just to sit there, pretending that everything was all right. I didn't dare tell Jackson I thought I was crazy. That probably would have freaked him out. I was so miserable; I said a silent prayer. *Lord, I don't want to die. Please help me. Why can't I date like everyone else? Why is this invisible monster trying to take over my life?* I didn't want to be different; I just wanted an answer. Unfortunately, I didn't know who to ask.

Eventually, we arrived in Atlantic City. When we went into the bar and restaurant, the first thing Jackson wanted was a drink. I probably needed a drink too. I was shaking like a leaf. The fear I encountered was overwhelming. I noticed that there were areas where he and I were incompatible.

Despite how friendly Jackson was, he was tight with money. Once, when Jackson took me shopping, I was a nickel short for an item I wanted to purchase. I asked, "Jackson, could you loan me a nickel? I'll pay you back when I get to my apartment." I tested the water. I paid the nickel back. It surprised me when he took it. This man is cheap, I thought. Although Jackson respected me in other ways, I didn't realize until later that he was going to the bar every night when he left my apartment. When it came to drinking alcohol and going to church, we were not compatible. I enjoyed going to church. He enjoyed going to bars. He didn't take me to bars, nor did he go to church with me. I prayed that maybe one day I could convince him to go to church.

I was so happy when Jackson took me to our hotel room. We got away from the crowd that had gathered in the bar and restaurant. The hotel was not the best-looking hotel I had seen, but I was more concerned about having those awful feelings with the door closed. Thank God we only spent one night there. Atlantic City was nothing like I'd imagined it to be. The boardwalk was run-down. The city looked like it needed repairs. It was winter, so there weren't many people walking on the boardwalk. The cold air brushing up against my face as Jackson and I took a long walk on the boardwalk was like a dose of medicine helping me cope with managing my fears.

Thank God we left Atlantic City at night. I didn't have to worry so much about Jackson noticing the way I was acting. Driving at night, Jackson focused his attention more on driving than on me dealing with those feelings. My body grew tired. The more I had to fight back against that monster, the stronger it became. It wouldn't let go. I was fighting something invisible, and only I could feel it.

When my phone rang one evening around seven o'clock, I just knew it was Jackson calling me. We had been dating for almost a year, and he had not missed a day of calling me around that time. When I answered the phone, to my surprise, it was his father. Right away, he told me that someone had mugged Jackson at a bar in Newark. I wanted to know what happened and why he was at a bar that time of the evening. The mugger had broken one of Jackson's arms and legs. That meant he would be incapacitated for a long time. I wanted to see him right away. Jackson's father took me to see him, but he didn't know the entire story about who mugged him. I couldn't help but be suspicious that he had gotten into a fight with someone at the bar because the mugger took nothing of value from him. I never found out the whole truth. Jackson said someone mugged him, and he left it at that.

Jackson was disabled for almost a year, unable to use his hand or leg. He became depressed. I could see we were drifting apart. His attitude was not the same, and he got upset over little things. Jackson knew as well as I that the phone company was not a part of my future. It was too stressful, and my transfer to another location had been denied twice.

When I told Jackson I had plans to go back to school, he wasn't happy. He asked, "Why do you want to go back to school? You have an excellent job working at the phone company." I don't know why he got upset when I told him that my dream was to become a secretary. He and I both knew that would never happen for me at the phone company. I went to a computer programming school two nights a week, taking computer programming classes. Before going to class, I would stop by to see Jackson. The school was about two blocks from where he lived in East Orange.

One day, he had such a bad attitude that we broke up. It was a big fight over nothing. I was turned off when I tried sitting next to him to cheer him up. When I asked if he was okay, he snapped at me and pushed me away from him. When I asked if he wanted me to continue to see him before I went to class, he didn't give me a straight answer. He said, "Do whatever you want to do." I felt uncomfortable with that answer. So, I told him I would never come by again. And that's what I did.

Later, I understood that his injuries and his inability to do the things he used to do caused his behavior. Unfortunately, I couldn't deal with it. My focus was on going back to school. I didn't see him anymore. However, after only six months, I quit school. I realized that being a computer programmer was not for me. I wanted to do secretarial work. When Jackson came to his senses, he called me to reconnect, but the chemistry was no longer there for me. The trust had diminished. I thought he was almost a perfect gentleman, but I was afraid that the behavior he exhibited the day we broke up might happen again. Trust was important to me, and Jackson had broken that trust.

A New Life: Business School

I ignored the girls in the office at the phone company when Peter and I became friends. I saw the jealous looks on their faces. I didn't let that bother me; in fact, I thought it was hilarious. I understood why Peter attracted the girls. He was a pleasant, good-looking guy. Well dressed, masculine, charming, and outgoing. He came into the office every day to pick up work. For some reason, he talked to me but not the other girls. I went out to lunch with him sometimes, but we never dated. I could tell him almost anything, but I couldn't tell him my secret.

Peter was one reason I began taking night classes at Essex College of Business. When I told him I wanted to go back to school, he took me to register for night classes. I liked that the school was only two blocks from my job. I went after work three nights a week, from 6:00 p.m. to 9:00 p.m.

I was determined not to let that invisible monster interfere with going back to school and fulfilling my potential. When class ended, I wouldn't take a bus. It was perilous to travel at night, and I was concerned that riding the bus home alone might trigger fear and that unpleasant feeling. People were most vulnerable to robbers and muggers at night, in the dark. Every night after class, I took a taxi. That way I not only arrived home quicker, but I avoided the feelings that made me anxious.

I thought I had everything under control, but one night I was in English class when suddenly I could not breathe. The classroom was small and crowded. It had never been that full. I left the class abruptly because I couldn't concentrate, and I was losing control. Once again, the invisible monster was taking over my life. I became fearful of being exposed. What would the other students think? What would my professors say if they realized there was something wrong with me? I couldn't handle the thought of that, so I dropped out of class. I cried my eyes out because I enjoyed going to night school. I felt like I was on my way to living out my dream. This was the second time I had tried to go back to school to become a secretary and didn't complete my course. I was hurt and disappointed. In three months, I could have graduated. I was determined that no matter how much that invisible monster interfered with my dream, I would become a secretary.

My sister was a member of First Timothy Baptist Church, and soon after I moved to New Jersey, I became a member too. I liked how the worship services were like my church down south. I felt at home because most of the members were originally from the South, having moved to New Jersey to seek employment. It was a much larger church than the one I belonged to back home. I sat in the pew with my sister at the front of the church. My secret was safe.

One Sunday, while the pastor was delivering his message, out of nowhere, the invisible monster attacked me again. It was like what happened that night I was in class. I got up and went outside into the vestibule to get some air for a few minutes. When I returned inside, I sat in the back of the church. Sitting behind people, I felt I could escape if I needed to. For a long time, I sat in the back of the church until eventually I stopped attending. Most of the time, the church would be full, and being around a crowd of people made me feel uncomfortable.

My sister never questioned why I started sitting in the back, but after that episode, I worried I'd have another one at church. I would always go to the altar for prayer. I whispered the same prayer I wrote in my diary. When I told the pastor I had a problem breathing, he did a special prayer with me. I was too ashamed to tell him the truth. I felt God knew what was wrong, and He was going to heal me. I'm not saying God didn't hear me. However, I continued having those unpleasant episodes in church.

Am I Crazy? The Doctors

Dr. Smith was Jackson's family doctor, and I continued to see him as my primary doctor after Jackson and I broke up. While we were dating, Jackson suggested I go see his doctor. "I'm sure he can help you with your sinus problem." I knew it wasn't my sinuses, but I couldn't bring myself to tell him that my problem was riding in a car. I wasn't sure if a physical doctor could help me, but I made the appointment to satisfy him.

The day I walked into Dr. Smith's office, I was praying for a miracle. Dr. Smith was white, well built, masculine, and probably in his late fifties. His office was near Jackson's home. I liked his personality right away—he seemed more concerned about my problem than most doctors I had been to. Jackson had told me that Dr. Smith did not rush seeing his patients, and that was true. He talked to me for almost an hour before he examined me. He wanted to know everything about my medical conditions and my life history. I talked to him about everything—except the sexual assault I'd experienced. I was still in suppression mode. I was also afraid to tell him I had an intense fear of losing control and I felt like I was going to die.

I thought, *If I tell him about the strange feeling, I know he's going to tell me I'm losing my mind.* I was praying he had the answer to my problems after all those tests he had ordered. The result of the tests was not what I was expecting to hear. I was diagnosed with iron deficiency anemia. Dr. Smith prescribed iron pills to take for a while. He wanted me to increase my dietary intake of iron-rich foods to help improve my iron levels. I was not too fond of one thing Dr. Smith prescribed. He said, "I suggest you drink a glass of wine every day with your dinner. It will help increase your iron level."

I told him I never had drunk alcohol before and had mixed feelings about drinking wine. I was raised to think that drinking alcohol and smoking were sinful. If people in my community knew I was drinking wine, they would condemn me. Most everyone I knew didn't drink alcohol or smoke. I heard a lot of people in the North say, "If you invited someone to your house in the South, they would offer you food but no alcohol. In the North, it's the opposite."

It took me a couple of days to decide to take the doctor's advice about the wine. I felt I had no other choice if I wanted to improve my iron levels. In addition, I was praying the wine would take those strange feelings away from me. Preston, one of my coworkers that had not been working long at the phone company, bought it for me. We were friends, just like Peter and I. Preston was a good-looking man. He was from Ohio. Unlike Peter, he was dark, medium build, and handsome. I told Preston the doctor had prescribed me to drink a glass of Manischewitz wine every day with my dinner and asked him to buy it for me. It was no big deal to him because he drank like a fish every day. Most of our coworkers thought he had a problem with alcohol.

I had no clue what I was doing. I tried imitating drinking wine the way I had seen it in television commercials. I placed ice into a large wineglass. Instead of sipping the wine slowly, I drank it like a glass of water or soda. Immediately, my head started spinning like a top. I was so dizzy. I started crying and talking crazy. Scared, Preston left and went home. He didn't want my sister to blame him for getting me drunk. That was an unpleasant experience. Suffice it to say, I didn't drink any more of that wine. I poured it down the kitchen sink. But I took the iron medication.

In hindsight, I blame myself for not being truthful with the doctors about the first time I experienced the feeling of losing control while riding in my father's car, in my landlord's apartment, and the episode I had on the bus that day on my way home from work. If I had told the doctors and my family sooner, perhaps I could have coped with it better. To alleviate my guilt, I often tell myself that back then, what I was experiencing was unheard of by most people. I'm not sure anyone could have helped.

When I realized that Dr. Smith was not helping with my problem, I went to see another doctor. The invisible monster was now attacking me at work. The stress level at my job was increasing more and more each day. One day at work, I was sitting at my desk when suddenly my chest tightened, and I couldn't breathe. By the time I reached my supervisor to explain what I was experiencing, I could barely see anyone in the office. I was weak and nervous. My supervisor could see how dizzy I was by the way I was wobbling. I was losing control. She didn't know what to do. She took me to the conference room, and I sat on a chair until I calmed down. She called my sister to come and take me home. I was still too embarrassed to tell anyone about the sudden intense fear of dying and feeling like a monster was choking me. My sister and everyone at work thought it was just from the stress of the job.

That evening, I went to see Mattie's doctor. She recommended him highly. She had been going to him for years. I was lucky that he had an opening to see me right away, even though it was after office hours.

Dr. Hardy impressed me. He was only the second Black doctor I had ever visited. Back home, we had only one Black doctor in my area. Dr. Hardy was young, probably in his late forties. Just like Dr. Smith, he ordered a series of tests. The results came back negative. Thank God my iron level was better. I was not truthful with him either. He only knew what happened at work, but I did not tell him about my situation in detail. I led him to believe it was stress related to my job. He took me at my word, gave me valium to deal with the stress, and I hoped it would help my problem. It did not help with the stress at work, and it didn't take away my problem.

I soon realized that every time I went to work, the invisible monster was there interfering. Fear overwhelmed me. I felt like I was suffocating. I made lots of trips to the bathroom to escape to get air. I was suffering so much with these experiences; the doctor put me on a two-week leave of absence. Because I received sick pay, the doctor from my job had to examine me. I knew the doctor would not solve my problem when he repeatedly said I could go back to work. He never examined me. All he did was ask questions not related to my situation. Like "How are you feeling? Do you think you can go back to work tomorrow?" I kept telling him about my stress, although I didn't reveal the whole truth. It didn't matter; he just wanted me to go back to work.

The final time I went to see the company doctor was the last straw. I was on a leave of absence for two weeks at Dr. Hardy's request.

It was a Friday, and the company doctor wanted me to return to work that Monday. I said, "My doctor is on vacation for two weeks; I need his approval before I can go back to work." The company doctor disagreed.

Instead, he demanded that I go back to work right away, but I was too afraid to go back to work without Dr. Hardy's approval. I was so fearful of having the invisible monster controlling my life. I felt I had no other choice but to resign. Sooner or later, I probably would have resigned anyway. My problem progressively got worse. I continued to see Dr. Hardy for a while until I realized he couldn't help me.

Starting Over Again 10

The invisible monster continued to reoccur. Fear paralyzed me living in that apartment in Mattie's house. My sister wanted to know what was wrong with me because I was acting so strange. I told her the apartment was too small and that I wanted to move. I never told her what I was experiencing. My sister could no longer deal with the way I was acting, so she agreed to move into a larger apartment. She had no other choice because I was getting on her nerves daily. We went to a realtor to find another apartment.

After we had chosen our new apartment, we were surprised to discover that our cousin Bernadette owned the place we had picked out. She was one of our oldest cousins from the South who had lived in New Jersey for a long time. I went to school with her younger brother and sister. Bernadette lived in the South Ward—one of the nicest neighborhoods in Newark. I was sure moving into a more prominent place would eliminate the invisible monster that had been a thorn in my side. There was no doubt in my mind that things were going to be better.

One hot and sweaty night, when I was home alone, I went to sit in the living room to cool off and watch one of my favorite TV shows. That old familiar feeling crept back into my life, and I suddenly couldn't breathe. The air conditioner was in the bedroom window next to the living room. Still, the air was not circulating throughout the apartment. I felt faint. "Oh no!" I said out loud. This couldn't be happening. Not again. I was so afraid; I didn't know what to do. My sister was hundreds of miles away. She had gone to visit our parents in North Carolina. I needed air. When I went outside to sit on the front porch, my cousin Bernadette was sitting in a chair on her side of the duplex looking at me strangely.

She asked if I was okay. I didn't tell her the truth about the strange feeling. Instead, I said, "I'm not feeling well. I need some air. I can't breathe. I'm sure I'll be okay soon." She insisted on taking me to see a doctor. I told her I didn't want to go to the doctor. I knew seeing a doctor wouldn't help my situation. I'd been there and done that so many times. It was a waste of time, I thought. She calmed down when I said it was my sinuses but insisted that I see the sinus doctor whose office was several blocks from where we lived. She said, "He's a good doctor." Even though I had reservations about going to another doctor, I made an appointment anyway.

For years, I had some problems with my sinuses, but not to where I needed to see a doctor. And these experiences were like my sinus problem. When my nose was stuffy, I couldn't breathe, nor could I breathe when I had these attacks. I thought maybe my sinuses could have caused my problem. I hoping that was the answer to my prayers. I thought, What the heck? I'll let him examine my sinuses; it might help eliminate my problem.

I didn't tell this new doctor about the invisible monster either. Dr. Groves was a young white man. I was grateful he gave me a thorough examination and was attentive to my concerns. But I knew if I didn't come clean, the visit would be all for nothing. Unless, of course, I had other medical problems besides my sinuses.

It scared me when the nurse came into the examination room and said the CT scan was incomplete. I said, "Oh God, they have found the problem, but it's not going to be good." The nurse could see how frightened I was. I had a scared look on my face. I was very nervous and anxious while talking to her. She said, "Calm down, Ms. Parker. I must retake the CT scan. I don't know why the other nurse took the CT scan with your wig on. You are going to have to take off your wig." I didn't braid my hair that day, so I'd just thrown a wig on. I'd used a bobby pin to hold it in place. The bobby pin was interfering with the reading of the CT scan. I hesitated when I pulled my wig off in front of the nurse, but the nurse was more concerned about the CT scan than she was seeing my hair standing on top of my head. The reading was normal. I breathed a sigh of relief that nothing serious was wrong with my head; however, I was a little disappointed that they had found nothing. At least if they had found a medical condition, I might have gotten some answers about my issue.

The doctor also ordered an allergy skin test to find out what was causing my sinus problems. The specialist put a drop of the suspected allergen on the surface of my skin. The test was performed on my back and forearm. I had a positive reaction to so many things, including dust and mold. So even though I felt my problem wasn't physical, I was sure when he cleaned out my sinuses, it would help with my breathing. I don't remember what he used to clean out my nose, but it felt like a long, thin stick. He pressed so hard that I still have sensation from that spot today. "This hurts so bad!" I screamed. He just said, "This is what I must do to clean your sinuses." But, of course, this did not get rid of the invisible monster. So, I stopped seeing the doctor. It was just a waste of time and money I couldn't spare.

I hoped that one day, just maybe, one of those medications would solve my problem. But one morning, I woke up and could barely see. It was like a white web covered my eyes. I used Visine eye drops, hoping that would help. Instead, my eyes were getting worse. This scared me to death. I went to East Orange to see an ophthalmologist right away. At first, I couldn't understand Dr. Chucks's African accent. But then I heard him say after he examined my eyes that I was about a minute away from going blind. I didn't have to ask him to repeat it twice. He knew the problem: I had taken so many medications from different doctors that it had affected my vision. I trashed the grocery bag full of ineffective medicines, and my eyes returned to normal, but it did take eighteen months.

Keep Fighting

With no friends, no boyfriend, and no job, all I did all day was sit in my room, watch TV, write in my journal, have pity parties, and feel sorry for myself. I was too afraid to go anywhere. My sister had purchased a beautiful yellow Thunderbird. Sometimes she wanted me to go shopping with her at the mall. I always had an excuse. I led her to believe I wasn't feeling well, or I'd go another time. I was too embarrassed to tell her I couldn't ride in a car, especially on the parkway. I did manage to ride to church and go food shopping with her. But a lot of days, I sat in my apartment looking out the window, watching people walking up and down the street laughing and talking. I couldn't help but wish I could be just like them. Night and day, I prayed, seeking an answer to my problem.

After I resigned from the telephone company, I was too fearful of looking for another job. I knew I had to come up with a plan before my savings ran out. I thought about going back down south to live with my parents until I got myself together. But I didn't want to leave my sister without telling her the whole truth that I was suffering from more than the overwhelming stress I was experiencing at work. And I didn't want to be labeled as crazy because I could not work. My only alternative was to go back to school. I reapplied to Essex College of Business. I prayed that the invisible monster wouldn't reoccur and cause me to quit school again. In the meantime, I received unemployment. It wasn't enough to pay for school and other expenses. To help make ends meet, I took out a student loan. Drawing unemployment meant I had to look for work, but to be honest, I was hoping I could finish the nine-month course before I got a job.

I had some free time before school started, so I went home to see my parents for two weeks. I knew the bus ride would be miserable like it was the last time I rode the bus with my sister when we went home to attend Dorothy's mother's funeral.

The day I left for my two weeks' vacation, I was so eager I was going home to see my family until I took a taxi to the bus station. On the ride there, I was losing control, worrying that the bus ride would be as miserable as it was last time.

I attended Dorothy's mother's funeral because I will always believe in my heart that she did all she could to convince her daughter to testify about that night. I didn't hesitate to go to her funeral, even though I knew the bus ride going home and coming back to Newark would not be pleasant. I took the chance. The day my sister and I left for the funeral, I worried I would have to deal with the invisible monster on the bus. Fear propelled me, and my anxiety was through the roof. If I said anything to my sister about those feelings, she would have thought I was crazy.

My sister slept the entire eight hours, both going and coming back on the bus. I wanted to go to sleep, but I couldn't. I was fighting too hard to keep that monster off my back. When I got off the bus, it was a joy to relax and breathe in the fresh air.

As I was getting on the bus to go down south, I had an emotional flashback when my sister and I went to Dorothy's mother's funeral. It was like a ride to hell when this feeling crept up on me. I was miserable, wanting to get air, and anxious. I was sorry I had told my family I was coming home for two weeks. When the monster started attacking me, I overheard the lady sitting across from me talking to her friend about how many times I had gone to the bathroom. I must have gone ten times. She thought I was sick, but I was having trouble breathing. Occasionally, I felt like screaming at the bus driver to stop the bus. I thought I was going to die. I didn't feel any relief until the bus stopped in Washington, D.C., to dislodge and load passengers. I knew I was halfway home, which helped me manage some of my fears and anxiety.

When I got off at the bus station in North Carolina, I felt like I had been riding a rollercoaster. I was so glad to see my father when he picked me up in Greenville, but I was a nervous wreck.

I thought my secret would be safe if my family believed I was suffering from motion sickness. Most people know motion sickness is a common thing, and nobody deems it crazy. I let my family believe that partial truth for years. I didn't want to tell a lie when I confessed to my family about the miserable bus ride, but it was easier than telling them the truth.

While I was home, I found out that my cousin Marion and her husband, Bob, were visiting her mother. Bob was stationed at Fort Dix, New Jersey. It was a coincidence they came home at the same time I did. My mother was so happy.

She said, "Since you get motion sickness riding the bus, you should ask Marion for a ride back to New Jersey!"

If I had told the truth, my mother would have known I had just as much fear riding in the car as I did on the bus. I was between a rock and a hard place. But I took the ride, hoping I'd do better in a car than I did riding home on the bus.

The day I left to go back to New Jersey with my cousin and her husband, my little niece Louise, and nephew, Darnell, didn't want to see me go. My niece and nephew ran beside the car crying until we were out of sight. I wanted to cry along with them because I knew I had to endure the long trip cooped up.

The ride back to Newark with my cousins was everything I expected it to be. I had trouble breathing. I tried closing my eyes to go to sleep, but sleep didn't come. My cousin stopped at rest areas a couple of times when I said I had to go to the bathroom. I didn't have to use the bathroom. I just needed some time to take a break. I stood inside the bathroom against the wall, praying. I asked God to give me the strength to make it to Fort Dix.

It was late when we arrived in New Jersey, and I spent the night at my cousin's house; I planned to take the bus the following day to Newark. The bus ride was not as long, but I still suffered from those feelings. When I got to Newark, I told myself that I would never ride on a bus again. I was frustrated dealing with that invisible monster.

I felt like my life was ending. I became extremely depressed. I didn't know how to deal with it anymore. I couldn't ride on a bus or in a car or be around a crowd of people. I felt like I couldn't live my life! I left the house only to go to church. I completely stopped associating with anyone. I prayed for healing, but it seemed like God was not listening to my prayers. The only comfort I got was when I wrote in my journal. That was my way of expressing my emotions and communicating my secret.

I started attending Essex County College of Business (ECB) soon after I came back from visiting my parents. One day in my typing class at ECB, I noticed the girl sitting next to me watching how fast I was typing. Immediately, I stopped typing, looked at her, and smiled. She returned the smile. Then she said, "My name is Annette. I was admiring how fast you type. How did you learn to type that fast?"

I said, "I practice every day." I had purchased an electric typewriter back when I was going to school at night. Having a typewriter at home helped me gain speed without looking at the keyboard. When I reached my goal of typing one hundred words per minute, I was proud. I was the fastest typist in my class.

Annette and I hit it off right away. We became Best Friends Forever (BFFs.) Sometimes we would be on the phone talking for two hours. We were both from North Carolina. She'd grown up an hour away from my hometown. People often thought I was Annette's daughter because she was tall and I was so short, but Annette was only three years older than me. She also lived in Newark's South Ward. We were not that far from each other. Both Annette and I were in our late twenties and talked a lot about everything. Unfortunately, I couldn't bring myself to tell her about my secret. We had a lot in common. When we rode the bus together after class, we talked until we reached her bus stop. All that talking helped with the hyperventilation that made me feel suffocated when I rode the bus.

I met another young woman during this time. Her name was Penny. Penny dressed differently than the other people in school. Every day she had on a long dress, thick stockings, and a black hat. Right away, I knew she dressed that way because of her religious beliefs—some people in my hometown dressed in that manner. Later, I learned that she and her family were members of a holiness church. At lunch one day, Penny said, "Mary, I'd like for you to meet my brother Jesse. I know he will like you." I hesitated before I said anything. I thought it was a joke.

Annette said, "You don't have a boyfriend; I think it's a great idea." I don't know why she chose me out of all those girls in my class. I took my time before I agreed to meet him.

My Next Love: Jesse

Jesse and I hit it off right away. I thought he was so sexy and handsome—just my type. I've always found men who are a few inches taller than me attractive. I thought he was my knight in shining armor. Since Jesse did not have a car, that meant I didn't have to worry about riding in one when we went out on dates. But I had to worry about taking a bus or train. Jesse mostly took public transportation when he visited me.

Things went well until Jesse and I visited his friend in Holland, New York. We took the train and subway, but I didn't want to tell him I felt like I was suffocating riding on the train. I knew it was going to be a problem, but I went anyway. Immediately, I was afraid. I desperately tried to pretend everything was okay. Thank God the train ride wasn't that long from Newark to New York. But when we got off the train, we took the subway to his friend's apartment. It was a blessing in disguise when we finally got off the subway and were able to get some fresh air as we walked down the street.

That day, Jesse and I dressed to kill. He wore a white shirt trimmed in gold with matching white pants trimmed in gold on the side. I had on my black pantsuit trimmed in white. We had everyone's attention on and off the train. As we walked down the street, people driving in their cars slowed down to compliment us. I enjoyed the visit to New York. But by the time I returned home, I was shaking all over. It was a miserable ride going to and from New York, and Jesse could sense something was wrong. He asked, "Are you feeling okay?" I told him I was having trouble with my sinuses, and sometimes it was hard to breathe.

I cried myself to sleep that night because I didn't know if I could continue the relationship. I didn't know how much longer I could cope with the fear of riding on the train or bus every time we went on a date.

It was extremely frightening. When Annette and Penny asked me how it was going, I pretended I was having a ball. I didn't want to reveal my secret.

The monster attacked me one day when Jesse touched me. We were at his parents' house alone. Out of respect, I didn't want to make love at his parents' house. He pulled me into his arms and wouldn't let me go when I refused to make love. He didn't want to take no for an answer. He kept pulling on me and pinned me down on the bed. No matter how many times I tried to get away, I couldn't escape. He was acting like a wild person. I had never seen him that aggressive before. Something triggered inside me: I thought he was trying to rape me. I started to scream, "Don't touch me like that!" He was so frightened. He thought I was losing my mind. I finally calmed down. It had been almost ten years since the night I was raped. No matter how hard I tried to overcome that night, it still haunted me if a man touched me in that manner.

Jesse stopped and pulled me into his arms. He saw how frightened I was. He apologized over and over and promised that it would never happen again. I believed him. He was true to his words. It never happened again. We continued dating, and I became more comfortable being around him. He came from a friendly, religious family. When I met them, they embraced me like I was a part of the family. I hated that Jesse and I had different religious beliefs—he was raised under the apostolic faith of Bishop Johnson while I was Missionary Baptist. We didn't have dress codes. I let Jesse know from the beginning that I would not change my dressing style. There was no way I was going to wear a hat all the time with a long dress and thick stockings like his sister Penny. But out of respect for his mother, I wore a dress when I visited him.

I was so sorry I went with Jesse to his church headquarters in Philadelphia for their yearly celebration. That's when all the churches came together from all over the states. I knew it was going to be a miserable two-hour ride to and from Philadelphia. One of Jesse's younger brothers drove his car. That was a good excuse for me to sit in the back seat while Jesse sat in the front with his brother. I was so miserable; it was difficult for me to communicate. I didn't hide my reactions from Jesse's brother. He could see how I was cringing in the back seat. I lied when he asked if I was okay. I said I needed to go to the bathroom. But when he offered to take me some place to use the bathroom, I didn't want to prolong the time getting there any longer. I just wanted to get to the church as fast as we could. I needed air. We were already two hours late trying to find the church.

When we arrived at the church, the only available seats were in the back, which didn't bother me. The long ride had made me nauseous, dizzy, and nervous. The sanctuary was massive—it probably held over five hundred people, which made me uncomfortable. I wasn't focusing on what was going on. I just needed some air. I told Jesse I was sick. He took me to the basement of the church. I was so happy that I could escape all those people.

The services lasted all night. Jesse wanted to stay for the entire thing. I just wanted to go home. I was lucky to get a ride back from Philadelphia with Jesse's cousin. I left Jesse there. The ride back was just as miserable. I had no other choice but to sit in the front seat with Jesse's cousin because some members were already sitting in the back when I got into the car. I tried so hard to compose myself. Once in a while, Jesse's cousin wanted to know if I was okay when she noticed I was gasping for breath. I said, "I'll be fine. I need some sleep." I was so glad when we reached Jersey City. I took the train home. Once I got into my apartment, I breathed a huge sigh of relief. I made a promise that I would never go to Philadelphia with Jesse again.

Before graduating from Essex School of Business, I went to New York from Newark's Penn Station. Ms. Henderson, one of the teachers, took some of the class to the city to apply for jobs. When we got off the train, we had to take the subway to the World Trade Center. That ride was just as miserable as riding on the train, and of course, I had those familiar feelings.

Although I knew I would suffer riding the train, I did things I knew would be a problem for me. I was not going to let that invisible monster prohibit me from getting a job. I was going to make my life work, no matter how difficult it was. I thought, *the ride is less than thirty minutes. You can do it.* I didn't want to tell my classmates I had a problem riding on the train. Especially Ms. Henderson. She had high hopes I would pass the test. I prayed I could pull it off.

On the ride, I sat with Annette. All I could do was try to act normal while she was talking to me. No one had a clue how much I was suffering. I don't know how I did it, but when I got to the office, a classmate and I nailed the typing test. We were the only two people in the class who passed the test, and we were each offered a job working for a magazine company. I wasn't expecting to get a job just like that. I knew I couldn't reveal my secret, so I came up with an excuse that I didn't enjoy working in New York. In my heart, I knew it would be a problem for me to take a bus, train, and subway every day to and from work. It broke my heart that I couldn't take the job because I needed it desperately. My unemployment was running out.

When I told Ms. Henderson I would not accept the position, she was somewhat disappointed. But when the other student accepted the position, she felt that going to New York was not in vain. Occasionally, I would run into my classmate, and she told me she liked her job. I am sure I would have, too, especially since I would've been working with someone I knew from class. But I didn't give up hope that I would find a job working in Newark.

The night I graduated from ECB, my classmates were putting on their robes in the dressing area, and the invisible monster showed up. As soon as I got into the room, everyone wanted me to take pictures. I snapped at them and said, "No. I don't want to take any pictures." I regretted my tone, but I couldn't tell them what I was experiencing. The room was small and tight, and I couldn't breathe. The door was closed, and I needed air. I had on my cap and gown and had been looking forward to this day. I calmed down when I left the room.

Jesse was proud of his sister and me when our names were called to receive our diplomas as executive secretaries. My sister took me to the graduation, but I spent the night with Jesse and his family. His mother owned a restaurant, and we celebrated there.

After graduation, I saw the type of person Jesse really was. We had lots of fights. Jesse like to take control over all situations. He wanted everything to go his way. He didn't like to listen to my opinion or anyone else's. He was always right. When he tried to boss me around, I nipped it in the bud. He didn't like when I disagreed with him, but I stood my ground. This, as well as me refusing to change my religious beliefs proved to be the end of our relationship. Jesse told me suddenly that he didn't know if he could continue a relationship with someone who did not share his religious beliefs. That was a deal-breaker for me. There was no way I was going to dress like his sister or mother. I refused to wear a long dress, hat, and silk stockings every day. I liked wearing dresses, but I also liked wearing pants, and I wasn't going to give them up. Besides, the invisible monster was also interfering with our relationship. I never felt comfortable on a date. I was tired of wrestling with the monster every time we rode the train or subway. I concluded that Jesse was not the person I wanted to spend my life with. It hurt me when we broke up. In retrospect, it was for the best for both of us.

We were just not compatible. We couldn't overcome our varying religious beliefs or our arguments when he didn't want to listen to the truth when he was wrong.

13
Home is Where the Heart is

I thought a trip home to see my parents was a great idea to relieve some of the stress that had built up in my run-up to graduating from business school. It felt like the perfect time to take a trip before my unemployment benefits ran out. Although I promised myself that I would never ride the bus again, that was the only way I knew how to travel. My father came to Newark to ride with me to North Carolina on the bus because they were still under the impression that I suffered from motion sickness.

I don't know why I thought I could hide my reaction to being on the bus with my father when he was there with me. Right away, it felt like I was suffocating and my body was escaping. I couldn't breathe and I needed air. My father noticed the nervous look on my face. He was sure I was having trouble from motion sickness and tried to comfort me. I went to the bathroom as much as possible, but not like the last time. Somehow, I made the trip work, but it wasn't easy. I just wished I had dared to tell my father the truth. Back then, when someone acted strangely and it was beyond the doctor's capabilities, the first thing people would say was, "They must have a spell on them." I suspected the same thing. I didn't have a clue what I was dealing with. I knew it wasn't physical, so I assumed it had to be what other people were saying. Even if that were true, I wouldn't know how to get the spell off me. I was thrilled I was home with my family. But that was the last time I rode the bus going to and from New Jersey.

When my father saw how uncomfortable I was riding the bus, he thought it would be a great idea if I took the train back to Newark. I'd never ridden on an Amtrak train before. I was a little nervous. The Amtrak train was nothing like riding the train going to and from Jersey City or New York. I liked that I would have privacy in a sleeper car. I was so amazed when I saw the small roomette, built-in toilet, and a small bed. But I knew it was going to be a problem when I closed the door. I needed air. I couldn't breathe. I had the door open until the conductor came by to check my ticket. He said it was against their policy to ride in the roomette with the door open. I just ignored the conductor when he questioned why I paid extra money to ride just eight hours in a sleeper car. I don't know if he was serious or making a joke. I closed the door, hoping to have a smooth ride. I took out a word puzzle book, hoping that would help me stay focused. It didn't help much, but the train ride was somewhat better than the bus ride because I was not around people who might be looking and judging my reactions. When I was experiencing losing control, I couldn't eat, sleep, or rest for eight hours and was miserable until I got off the train.

 I would have never thought that the trip back to Newark would land me a job. As soon as I got into Mr. Henry's taxi, we began to talk. We talked until we reached my apartment. He said he was a manager with the Newark Housing Authority, that he was hiring, and I should apply. I went the next day. Although it was a temporary job, it didn't matter to me. I needed a job. Just as Mr. Henry predicted, I was hired. I applied to work in the payroll department. It wasn't an executive secretary position, which I had gone to school to become, but it was better than New Jersey Bell and was far less stressful. What I liked the most was that I only worked six and a half hours per day.

 My problem was that I had to take two buses to and from work. The first day I got off work, I walked to the bus stop to take the first bus, and I felt fine. As soon as I entered the second bus, there were no empty seats in the back. The bus was crowded. About halfway to my stop, I could not breathe. My heart palpitated, and I felt dizzy. *Oh God. No. I prayed. God, I need this job. Please help me.* The ride was about thirty minutes. I could not escape the invisible monster that was haunting me. Repeatedly, I said, *I need this job.* Even though I knew it was temporary, I was not about to quit. Every day I got off work, I thought about having episodes of intense feeling, just like I did when I worked at the phone company. I just persevered, no matter how difficult it was.

 I learned that I could get full benefits by taking the civil service exam to become a permanent employee. That was music to my ears. I immediately took it. The test was hard! It lasted for two hours. In the last part of the exam, I had to take a typing test. I wasn't aware I was being stared at by some of the workers who gave the test, but later they told me they were amazed at how fast I could type. I passed with flying colors.

Midnight Rides: The Monster Rises

The invisible monster was holding me hostage. It was like I was put into prison for a crime I did not commit. I wanted so badly to go with Annette, her sister Evelyn, and friends when she invited me to go for a ride. I always came up with an excuse because I was fearful of riding in a car. I would tell her I was too busy sewing, or I would go another time. Sewing was a perfect excuse because practically every time Annette called me, I was making an outfit. I'd taken a six-week-long sewing class and immediately put my new skill set to work making clothes for my family and me. That kept me motivated. Besides, I had to alter most of the clothes I bought.

Lenny and I became friends soon after I was promoted to the benefits department at the Newark Housing Authority. One day, he came into my office to fill out his health insurance form, and we talked for a long time. I could relate to him because we both were from the South. Lenny had moved from Virginia to New Jersey several years before me. He started working in the Architect Department soon after I got the job at the Housing Authority. My sister and I could always depend on him to help us with the repair work that needed to be done in our apartment. Lenny stuttered. He told me he'd had a speech impediment since he was a child. After we had been friends for a long time, I just tuned it out. His beautiful personality overshadowed his disability, and it did not affect his interaction with people. When my sister got married, he was a groomsman at her wedding. The bridesmaid he escorted thought he was so good-looking. He was tall and handsome.

The day my sister got married, Lenny noticed I was happy and sad. She and I had been together for a very long time, but I always knew that one day we were bound to separate from one another.

I helped my sister with planning her wedding. It was no surprise to me when my sister chose purple and white as her wedding colors.

Purple had always been her favorite color. On the day of her wedding, she looked so beautiful in her light beige wedding gown. Her light beige hat complemented her shape and height. I was one of the bridesmaids. I remember that the dress was purple, tea-length with long sleeves, but I don't remember every detail about the dresses. I prayed to God not to spoil my sister's day as I was getting in the limo to go to the church and the reception with the other bridesmaids. I couldn't help but think that I would be attacked by the invisible monster. But thank God, the seats in the limo had ample space between them. I could breathe with no problems.

Soon after my sister got married, Annette invited me to go on a midnight train ride to Montreal, Canada. I wasn't sure if I could take that long of a ride. Lenny encouraged me to take the trip. He said, "You need to get out of that apartment and socialize. You've been cooped up long enough." He knew I had trouble riding in a car, but he thought it was because of motion sickness. Lenny said I could take Dramamine pills for the motion sickness. Although nothing I'd tried had worked thus far, out of curiosity, I went to the drugstore and bought the Dramamine and took my deposit to the sponsor.

Annette was excited I'd decided to go on the trip. I wanted to go. It sounded like fun. I had never been on a trip outside the United States. My coworkers had asked me to go on a cruise with them to different countries, but I'd had to decline. I said I couldn't afford it. I felt that if I had problems riding in a car, on a bus, or a train, there was no way I could ride on a boat.

The train ride to Canada was called the Midnight Train to Canada. About one hundred people were boarding the train from the Newark Penn Station that night. Several train cars were reserved just for the tour group. I took a motion sickness pill an hour before I boarded the train, but as soon as I boarded and sat with Annette near the window, it was like the invisible monster set down between us. I couldn't breathe. I needed air. I wanted to get off the train, but somehow, I persevered. One of the train cars was a bar car. She and I went to the bar after we got settled. People were having fun, laughing, and talking. I soon had to leave and excuse myself. I said that I was sleepy and went back to my seat. I was glad when the motion pill kicked in. I could feel my eyes getting heavy as they made me drowsy. I was so relieved that I slept most of the eight hours to Canada and didn't have to deal with a miserable ride. After we got settled in our hotel room, we went shopping down the street from the hotel with the girls.

Annette's cousin, who lived in Canada, came by the hotel that night. She took us out for a tour of the town. I couldn't enjoy myself because the pill I'd taken had me so tired and sleepy. I really can't tell you what I saw! When we returned to the hotel, I fell asleep right away. The Dramamine was still in my system. I managed to keep my eyes open the next day when it was time for us to go on the bus tour. I didn't take a motion sickness pill that morning because I wanted to enjoy some of the trip. The tour lasted for about an hour. We stopped at so many places. We went to see a live basketball game that was already in progress at Notre Dame. We also went to a building that had just installed a glass elevator. Everyone was fearful riding on the glass elevator.

We left Canada at midnight. Just like I'd done on the way to Canada, I took one of the Dramamine pills an hour before boarding. I slept the entire trip back to Newark. But the motion sickness pills were too strong. All they did for me was make me sleepy. I couldn't bear living my life sleepily all the time, so I stopped taking the pills.

I decided that I was going to take more trips. I could not allow anxiety to rob me of my entire life. My church was planning a trip to Englishtown to go to a yard sale a church member was sponsoring. Right away, I thought, *No, you can't take that trip*. But I bought a ticket anyway. As I was boarding the bus that Saturday morning to Englishtown, the thought crossed my mind again, *You can't take the trip*. I ignored the voice until after I saw the bus was almost at capacity. I knew then I was headed for trouble. I had an emotional flashback to my experiences when I rode on crowded buses. It was difficult to be calm and act as though an invisible monster was not on my shoulder. I usually didn't go anywhere with the church. I'd surprised my sister and some of the members when I bought the ticket.

My sister rushed onto the bus to choose the middle seat so we could sit together. I wanted to sit in the back to avoid being around a crowd. As soon as the bus driver rode onto the parkway, my body slowly started to feel numb, and I became anxious. I tried to relax because I didn't want anyone to notice my behavior. But my sister did. She asked, "Are you okay?" I just lied and said I was okay. I was so sorry I went on the trip. I wanted to get off the bus. When we reached Englishtown, I rushed off the bus to get air. I stood in one spot for a while, praying to God to please release the monster that had just attacked me.

The place was so huge that I don't remember if we covered the entire area. We were there for most of the day. When it was time to board the bus, I dreaded the ride back. But I had no other choice. I couldn't walk back home. My sister and some members thought I was sick. I was gasping to breathe. I just said I was having a stomach problem. I probably wouldn't have taken the trip if I'd known the ride would be longer than an hour.

Several months later, the church went to see the Broadway play, *Mama I Want to Sing!* I had never been to a Broadway play before, and I didn't want to miss that opportunity, so I bought a ticket. The bus ride to New York was less than an hour. I was sure I could handle that distance. I was wrong. Riding over the bridge was where I thought I was going to jump out of my skin. Going through the tunnel was like I was having a nightmare with my eyes open. I thought I was going to die. I was happy that it was dark inside, so no one could see how I was acting.

Fortunately, I didn't have to ride back with the members after the play was over. I had made plans to spend the night in Brooklyn with my cousin Lenette. When the play was over, my cousin and her husband were there to pick me up. We took the subway to her apartment. I knew riding on the subway would be as tricky as riding on the bus or train, but it was a short ride. That night, my cousin's friend took us to Coney Island. A part of me wanted to say, "I don't want to go." I knew I couldn't take that ride, but I couldn't come up with an excuse not to go. Sure enough, as we were riding in the car to Coney Island, I started experiencing fear of being trapped inside. I wanted to escape. Once again, the invisible monster had attacked me. The ride was not that long, but it felt like hours. Because it was dark, no one noticed how much I was cringing in my seat. Mostly when riding in a car, I focused on things like fumbling in my purse or chewing gum to help me relax. When my visit was over, I took the train back to Newark. It was devastating riding the bus, car, and train. That entire experience was like I had gone to hell and back. I would never go on a church trip or visit my cousin again.

15

To Have and To Hold

On Mother's Day 1979, I met my husband. I went with Annette, her sister Evelyn, and Evelyn's friend Doris to dinner and a fashion show at one of the most exclusive places in Irvington, NJ. Unlike the other times Annette had invited me out, I didn't hesitate to accept her invitation. I knew the fifteen-minute ride in the car wouldn't be a problem for me. It was raining hard that day, and as soon as we arrived, I ran inside the building. I didn't want the white pantsuit I'd made especially for Mother's Day to get wet. It was a tradition for Black people to wear a white outfit or a red flower to represent their mother.

There were many people at the celebration. Doris introduced her cousin, Tommy, to us. He was short and handsome. He stood there staring at me, not saying a word for a while. I didn't know how to respond. Then he said, "Look what the Lord has sent me." The rest of the night was history. We talked for quite a while, and I found him to be very funny. I admired his personality right away. Later, I learned he was from Florida, and he didn't live too far from Doris. Before I left, he gave me his phone number. That was a good sign he wasn't in a relationship. He wanted my phone number; I didn't give it to him that night. I just said, "I will call you."

I had prayed that I'd meet someone nice to marry. It wasn't until later that I learned Tommy had prayed for the same. He was tired of dating and ready to settle down with someone nice. I hadn't been on a date in a year. Besides the tired feeling I was experiencing, I didn't want to socialize with anyone.

I gave Tommy a call about three or four days later. I could sense that he was surprised I called; we talked on the phone for almost an hour. Tommy told me he had never been married. Then he told me he was the second oldest child of sixteen siblings. I thought he was joking at first! It wasn't until later when I met all sixteen of his siblings, that I realized he was telling the truth. Tommy's oldest brother and a younger brother lived in New Jersey. Like me, he was raised in a Baptist church. He was Primitive Baptist, and I was Missionary Baptist. He had been employed at Ford Motor Company for about ten years. He talked about how he loved his job on the assembly line, attaching car doors. Before we went on our first date, I called Annette to ask her opinion. Although I felt comfortable talking to him on the phone since the first day, I still had doubts. I had so many challenges dating in the past, and it had been a while since I went on a date. Fear propelled me that something could go wrong. Annette insisted I go on a date with him. She said, "He's Doris's cousin. If he were a bad person, she wouldn't have introduced him to us."

Tommy took me to a drive-in movie. We saw *Night of the Living Dead*. Thank goodness, the ride wasn't that far from where I lived. I tried to relax while watching the movie, but as soon as Tommy parked the car, I knew it was going to be an awful night. As I contemplated being trapped in a car with the door closed, my body went into a fight-or-flight mood. I couldn't enjoy the movie. It was like a nightmare sitting in the car with all the doors closed. I wanted to leave. I came up with an excuse that made no sense so I wouldn't have to finish watching the movie. I tried to avoid Tommy asking me questions about the strange, intense reactions I was experiencing. He thought I was acting that way because I was afraid of what was happening in the movie. That was a perfect excuse. It didn't matter to him anyway because he wasn't into the movie and talked the entire time.

I hesitated when Tommy invited me to his apartment. Tommy had an efficiency apartment: one bedroom, a living room, and a walk-in kitchen. I was afraid to be there alone with him. *Suppose this guy tries to take advantage of me? I don't know him like that.* We sat in the living room watching TV. I tried to relax. I wanted to impress him, but I quickly pulled away when Tommy pulled me into his arms to kiss me. Immediately, I had a flashback to the night I was raped. I shouted, "Let go of me!" The more Tommy tried to calm me down, the more I tried to pull away. I was screaming, "Don't touch me like that! Take me home!" He tried to console me, but I ran to the door. I could tell that Tommy didn't know what to do. He had a confused look on his face. He calmly said, "I am not going to hurt you. Please sit down. I will take you home just to prove I am not going to hurt you." Whenever a guy touched me a certain way, it triggered a flashback. However, this incident didn't deter Tommy from going out with me.

The more time I spent with Tommy, the more the fear went away. He called every day. He was dependable and fun to be around. Tommy had to earn my sister's trust. It wasn't that she didn't like him, but we had just moved into another apartment. My sister wanted to make sure I wasn't inviting some guy there we couldn't trust. Tommy and my sister became very close. He always teased her and kept her laughing. That's the type of person he was when you first met him. He would say something to make you angry, then he would laugh and tell us he was joking. But once you got to know him, most people would laugh along with him when he told jokes.

The worst encounter I had with the invisible monster thus far was when I went shopping after work with Lenny. We went to Bayonne to buy his daughter some shoes, and I bought Tommy a Christmas gift. The mall was about a twenty-minute drive from my job. I felt like I could handle the ride, but we left during rush hour, when traffic was terrible. It was a nightmare riding in that heavy traffic. That prolonged the time I had to ride in the car. As soon as Lenny drove on the parkway, that's when the invisible monster revisited. Lenny was talking to me about his new job and noticed I wasn't responding as much as usual. He said, "You're getting carsick." I tried to play it off when Lenny said, "If those motion sickness pills are not working, it could be the type of food you're eating that's making you get sick like that."

I said, "That doesn't make any sense. I have a problem with riding. I don't have this problem when I eat." I didn't tell him I'd stop taking the motion sickness pills.

My heart was palpitating, and I thought I was going to die. I needed air. I asked how much longer the ride was, and Lenny said, "We're almost there." I wanted Lenny to stop the car, but I couldn't ask him to do that. Sometimes, when I was experiencing these strange feelings, I'd take out a piece of paper from my pocketbook and start writing, trying to stay calm. But that didn't help. I put the paper back into my pocketbook. All I could do was whisper a silent prayer. *Lord, please help me.*

When I got out of the car, there were sweat stains under my armpits—I was just that nervous. It took me a while to calm down. I told myself I shouldn't have come. I'd thought it was a perfect time to go shopping because I wouldn't have to take the bus home from work.

I dreaded the ride back. I felt some relief when Lenny took a shortcut to my apartment. Of all the times I'd experienced the invisible monster attacking me, this was the most difficult one. I prayed the same silent prayer. *Oh God, please help me.* I wanted Lenny to stop the car. My vision blurred, and I could barely see anything. I couldn't take it any longer. I didn't want to tell Lenny the extent of what I was experiencing. I said, "Lenny, I'm sick. I am going to sit on the floor." He had the seat pushed back because he had long legs. So, I had enough room on the floor to be comfortable the rest of the way home. But that didn't take away the frightening experience of feeling disconnected and out of control. I continued praying silently. *Oh God. I can't live like this. I need help. I'm so sorry I came. Just hurry and get me home.*

I rose off the floor and looked out the window. We were about five minutes away from where I lived. Lenny was talking to me, but I didn't know what he was saying. I just wanted to get home as fast as I could. Lenny rolled down the window because I needed air as I felt like I was losing my breath.

"Lenny," I said, "I have to do something about this situation. It's getting worse. I think I need to go see a psychiatrist."

He said, "Okay. But he can't do anything for you. I told you to see a nutritionist. It's probably the food you're eating." I knew Lenny was trying to help, but he didn't know what I was experiencing.

I said, "I'm going to call and make an appointment right away to see a psychiatrist. I need help." I left it at that.

I was shaking all over when I got home. I didn't care what Lenny said about going to see a psychiatrist. I needed mental health help. The invisible monster was more vicious and was now totally out of control. Any minute, I thought I was going to die. Instead of my problem getting better, it was getting worse every day. I didn't contemplate those feelings of fear riding the bus in the morning like I did in the afternoon. But now I must deal with breathing problems riding the bus mornings and afternoons. I was frustrated with that invisible monster chasing me every time I rode in a vehicle. This was the last straw. I felt I had no other choice but to seek help. All the mental health offices I called said I had to be referred by my medical doctor.

Dr. Drew was my medical doctor at the time. He referred me to see a psychiatrist when he understood that my problem was beyond something medical. At first, he thought I could take nerve pills to solve the problem, but I was persistent in my demands to see a psychiatrist. I am not sure a regular doctor could have diagnosed my problems. Thank God Dr. Drew referred me to a psychiatrist near where I lived. I didn't have to ride on the bus for a long time. Finally realizing my problem was not a medical one was a relief.

Although I was embarrassed to tell Annette that I was seeing a psychiatrist, I did it anyway. She didn't make me feel crazy when I told her, as I'd expected. Instead, she made me feel a lot better when she said she and her sister were also considering one. I did not expect Annette to reveal the reason she and her sister planned to visit a psychiatrist. We left it at that and ended the conversation.

When I told my sister and Lenny that I had made an appointment to see a psychiatrist, my sister said, "Huh." She was surprised. Her facial expression was all I needed to see. I didn't say another word. Lenny gave me negative feedback. I needed their support, but it wasn't there. However, this time I wouldn't let what others thought of me keep me from doing what was best for my life.

Seeking Help

On my first visit to Dr. Miller's office, I was nervous because I didn't know what to expect. All the psychiatrists I'd seen on TV were white men dressed in lab coats with solemn smiles on their faces. I must admit that when I saw Dr. Miller, I was very impressed—he was a tall, middle-aged Black man dressed in a suit. I was blown away. I didn't see a lot of Black doctors in my hometown, let alone a Black psychiatrist. Dr. Miller invited me to have a seat. I looked around for a sofa to sit on, but he was pointing to a chair. *This is not what I've seen on TV.* I'd expected to lie down on a sofa.

Dr. Miller sat across from me and grabbed his ink pen, writing a lot of information concerning my background. Looking back, I wished I had not still been suppressing the rape because that was something important I should have shared with him. I just started telling him about the episode of riding in the car with Lenny and the stress I was dealing with at my job.

. . .

My boss, Ms. Greene, was incompetent because she had little experience doing the assigned work. Most of the employees had a tough time working with her. I was heartbroken when I was assigned to her department in Family and Community Services. When my job had to downsize because of a mass layoff at the Housing Authority, the new director cleaned house. Most of the temporary employees were laid off. I had taken the civil service exam to become permanent just in time.

When my old boss, George, told us the Planning Department would be dissolved, I was devastated. I loved working in the Planning Department. I had finally landed my first secretarial job after I graduated from business school. I had a good boss. We worked well together. When I started at the Housing Authority, I worked in the payroll and benefits office, but I did clerical work. My desire to become a secretary was fulfilled.

The only thing I liked when I started working downtown was that I was close to my sister's job. That meant I could ride to and from work with her, and I didn't have to take the bus. This helped avoid some of the intense fear of having to deal with the invisible monster.

One thing I missed working in the Planning Department was my close friend Hester. He was such a nice guy who treated me like a sister. We talked about everything. But the one thing he never talked about was his sexuality, because he knew I was a religious person. I worked with lots of gay people. I treated everyone the same with love and respect. When I went to Essex County College and took music for a semester, Hester helped me play the piano. Before I purchased a piano, sometimes I would go to his house to practice. My music teacher told me I would never play the piano because my fingers were too small. Hester and I disagreed with that. The size of my hands didn't stop him from teaching me the notes. I was only interested in learning to play the piano. I never wanted to become a professional pianist. I learned to read notes and play better because Hester told me I should take private lessons. I took lessons for about two years.

Hester was brilliant. He helped me a lot when I became the union recording secretary. Before every meeting, Hester would proofread my minutes to make sure they were in the correct order. Even though I recorded the minutes and had a plan, they weren't easy to type. Sometimes the president or vice president had a difficult time calling the meeting to order. When the members were frustrated about a situation, they ignored the agenda and talked about the president. The parliamentarian was constantly calling the meeting to order. Hester and I were surprised when we both won the election to serve as officers. Hester resigned after serving as financial secretary for a year. He wanted to be the recording secretary.

I started as a receptionist when I was transferred to Family Services. I didn't mind because I sat at the front desk greeting office visitors. After I worked there for a while, things changed. I was assigned to work with Ms. Greene, who noticed my abilities. She decided I could do the head secretary's job. Because Ms. Greene didn't trust her assistant, Ms.

Harris, she never delegated much work to her. I found myself doing Ms. Harris's work and everyone else's work in the office. I was under tremendous stress when I was charged to supervise about ten youth during the summer. In addition, most of the workers Ms. Greene hired to assist me were inexperienced.

...

Dr. Miller had given me exercises on how to deal with stress during my first visit. It was like I went into a trance while he was talking to me. I don't remember why he gave me a picture to analyze as I stood by a closed door with my eyes closed. I remember writing how frightening it was when I did that part of the exercise in my journal. My hands began to slowly move up and down while he was talking to me. He said he wanted to see how well I could concentrate. I didn't quite understand what that meant, but I began to relax after that exercise.

It was like a miracle when he said I would be better within four or five weeks. And if that didn't work, he would try another method. I felt good about that. I just knew that was the answer to my prayer. Dr. Miller did not prescribe any medication; instead, he performed hypnosis exercises. I didn't believe in hypnosis, but the struggle I was encountering with the invisible monster made me willing to try anything I felt could help me.

During my next session, Dr. Miller put me through a relaxation exercise. I noticed he would talk and write simultaneously. I wondered if I was talking too much or if that's what you were supposed to do. I remember going into a trance before I was hypnotized. I looked at a spot on the wall, and Dr. Miller said, "When I count to ten, your eyes will get heavy."

He said different things like, "Sit up straight and put your hands flat on your lap." Finally, I was in a deep state of relaxation. I could hear him talking for a while, and then his voice faded. I couldn't open my eyes. I was in the relaxation period for a long time. Then I heard, "When I count to three, you will open your eyes." I felt so good when I opened my eyes. I wanted to fly around the room! When I left his office to take the bus home, I was still in a trance-like state, but I was aware of my surroundings and where I was going. I felt like I was coming down off a high. Also, I didn't have that fear I'd expected to face, as I did when I was riding the bus.

My appointments were scheduled during my work hours or after work. That meant I could not ride home with my sister. Three times a week, I took the bus. Ms. Greene let me have time off. She thought I was seeing a medical doctor. I dared not to tell her the truth.

I really can't say how much the sessions helped me when I went to see Dr. Miller on my last visit. I knew I wasn't completely free of the invisible monster. When I was leaving Dr. Miller's office, I said, "I will definitely use these exercises when I go on vacation next week."

He said, "Well, let me know how you make out. It was nice meeting you." We shook hands, and I thought I was on the road to recovery. Riding in cars was somewhat better but still not 100 percent great.

I tried to remember everything Dr. Miller said when I experienced breathing problems. I used the sayings to help counteract the fear. I could only remember that I had to close my eyes and concentrate on something pleasant. I had a problem with that exercise riding on the bus because I felt someone might snatch my purse if I closed my eyes for an extended time. I wanted to be constantly aware of my surroundings. In Newark, snatching people's pocketbooks took place all day, every day!

I took the morning train when I went on vacation, and I didn't have any problems whatsoever. The problems started after I arrived in the South. My sister Mae came to get me. I was going to stay with her for a while. As we were riding, I started having heart palpitations. I couldn't breathe. *Oh no! I thought I was over these feelings.* I tried to do the relaxation exercise. It was challenging to ride in the car. I didn't tell her how miserable I was. If I had told my family everything about my secret, it might have worked. During my entire trip and whenever I went on a long ride in the car with my family, I experienced problems with breathing and heart palpitations. Although I enjoyed being with my family, I didn't enjoy my vacation. I couldn't wait to get back to Newark to call Dr. Miller to tell him what I had experienced. I didn't know what to do. I didn't feel like a person anymore. I wanted to be like everyone else in my family, so I never gave up on prayer.

The day I got back from vacation, I called Dr. Miller. I said, "The exercises are not working. I still fear riding in a car. I guess it's something physical."

Dr. Miller said, "Oh no. It's not physical. Ms. Parker, come in to see me right away." I hung up the phone. I didn't know whether to jump out of a window or give up on life. I didn't know what to do anymore. Maybe I should just forget the whole thing. I was so disgusted.

Dr. Miller had me go through different types of relaxation periods. I was going once a week. It seemed to work for a while. Unfortunately, it didn't take away the intense feeling of losing control and feeling strange. I went to see him until I ran out of money. I could no longer afford to pay him forty dollars each week. That was a lot of money coming out of my paycheck.

Tommy made a joke when I said I was seeing a psychiatrist. He said, "Oh God, he might tell you I'm not good enough for you." I assured him it had nothing to do with him. If I could have continued seeing Dr. Miller, I would have gained enough courage to tell him the whole truth. It didn't bother Tommy that I saw a psychiatrist, but I didn't like it when he and my sister joked about me being crazy. It made me so angry because it was not a joke for me!

Although it wasn't a joke, people back then felt that way. You must be crazy if you went to see a psychiatrist. That is why I kept my secret. It took years before people understood that if you went to see a psychiatrist you were not crazy. I made a conscious decision that I would not see another doctor. I would handle my problem myself. I was looking for a miracle right away. Furthermore, I could no longer afford it.

17

Tommy's Secret

I noticed Tommy was somewhat disoriented and confused when he came to the front door to let me into his apartment. I asked Tommy, "Are you okay?"

He said, "I'm not feeling well. I'm going into the bedroom to lie down. I'll be okay in a few minutes. Just make yourself at home." Before I could get comfortable, I heard a strange gurgling sound coming from the bedroom. I nearly passed out when I saw it was Tommy making that strange sound. I walked closer to his bed, calling out to him. He didn't respond.

His body was jerking and shaking. Suddenly, he stiffened and lost consciousness. I didn't have a clue what was happening to him. I thought he was dying. I ran to the phone and dialed 911. In the meantime, I ran to the apartment next door, banged on the door, and cried out for help. The neighbor had no clue what to do either. Neither of us knew how to reach any of his family members. I'd met his older brother, Jake, and Jake's wife, Princess, but I didn't have Jake's work phone number, nor did I know where he worked. I remember Princess had said she was a manager at the New Jersey Bell telephone company in downtown Newark. I immediately dialed 411 to get the telephone number.

Princess knew right away what was wrong with Tommy. And she knew I was freaking out when I told her I thought Tommy was dying. She said, "Mary, calm down. I know what's wrong with Tommy. He is having a seizure." I said I had called 911. She said, "I am sure he won't need to go to the hospital once the paramedic examines him." Princess told me she had suggested to Tommy many times that he tell me he suffered from seizures. She knew it would freak me out if he had one in front of me. Tommy was carrying a secret just like me. I had never seen anyone have a seizure. I knew my father suffered from them after being discharged from the army, but I had never seen my father have a seizure because I lived in New Jersey when my father's seizures happened. When the paramedics arrived and examined Tommy, he had already regained consciousness. Just like Princess said, he refused to go to the hospital for treatment.

We both were off from work that day. We'd planned to spend some quality time with each other without any interruptions from his friends. When Tommy started feeling better, we ate dinner and watched TV until I went home.

Tommy worried that my seeing him have a seizure would end our relationship. However, I didn't break up with him. We had been dating for almost two years, and I had fallen in love with him. Tommy told me he had seizures about twice a year, but he could drive and go to work every day. It wasn't until later in our relationship that Tommy's seizures worsened because of alcoholism. I felt I could deal with his seizures far better than I could deal with my own problems. His was physical. He could take medication. On the other hand, I was suffering from a mental problem.

Married, but the Monster Lives

Tommy proposed to me on the sofa in the living room of his apartment in December 1983. I felt like a fish out of water when I put on the marquise-cut engagement ring. It didn't matter to me that there wasn't a lavish engagement party with family and friends. I loved him, he loved me, and that was all that mattered. Right away, I started planning to get married in six months. We didn't see any need for a long, drawn-out engagement. After all, we both were in our mid-thirties and had been dating for five years. Our families and friends were like broken records, constantly asking when we would get married. Tommy would just tune them out, but sometimes it annoyed me. However, when we announced our engagement, some of his family and friends jokingly said, "It's about time."

I wanted to have a June wedding, but all the places we chose to have our wedding reception were booked for June. That put a damper on my spirit, so we just settled for July 14, 1984.

My dream was to have a June wedding and to wear a long white wedding gown. Some of my friends teased me about wearing white because I was breaking the tradition. Back then, most people felt you should only wear white if you were a virgin. It didn't matter to me because I was planning my dream wedding. Although I was delighted about getting married, I knew I still had a weight on my shoulders. The only way I could get some relief was to tell Tommy everything about what I was experiencing. Fear held me back whenever I made up my mind to tell him the whole truth. I thought, *I'll be all right once we're married*. I pushed it aside and continued making wedding plans. I kept my fingers crossed and constantly prayed the heart pounding, can't breathe, fear of dying, and losing control would go away once I married.

It is normal to be stressed on your wedding day. However, my wedding day jitters were a combination of fear and stress because Tommy wasn't feeling well. It took him a while to get himself together before he put on his white tuxedo. Tommy and his groomsmen wore similar attire. Just before I got dressed, I was pacing around the apartment, saying a silent prayer. *Oh Lord, please don't let Tommy have a seizure, and don't let that invisible monster interfere with our wedding day.* Tommy could see I was stressed out. Over and over, he said, "Don't worry, Mary. It's going to be a wedding." I relaxed when Tommy felt much better, and his brother Jake came by the apartment to take him to the church. Jake was his best man.

 By the time the limo came to pick up my eight bridesmaids and me, I had calmed down. Everything was in order. It impressed me how smoothly the wedding ceremony went. Blue and white, representing faith, trust, and peace, were our wedding colors. My bridesmaids liked the long, low-cut blue dresses with ruffles around the short sleeves I chose. My blue and white flower bouquet, as well as the bridesmaids' bouquets in matching colors, were handmade by one of Annette's friends. Annette's friend suggested that I have my bouquet made large enough to keep a portion. I still have it today.

 I was disappointed that my father couldn't give me away as he'd promised. I accepted his apology when he said he couldn't come to New Jersey because his house was being renovated. Most girls look forward to having their father give them away, but it was an honor to have my brother be part of our wedding. As I walked down the aisle beside my older brother, David, I couldn't help but think about what my friends had said about me wearing a white gown. At that moment, I was just happy Tommy was feeling much better. It would have been devastating if we'd had to cancel the wedding. After all, we had invited more than one hundred family members and friends. As we stood under the arch saying our vows, I couldn't help but notice the beautiful decorations. The blue and white flowers hanging from the top and both sides of the arch were stunning.

 I met a lot of Tommy's siblings for the first time at the wedding. Unfortunately, not all his siblings could attend.

 I looked at the clock hanging on the wall. Our four hours for the reception were almost over. The last thing we needed to do was to cut the cake and throw the bouquet. The place was packed with our families and friends enjoying themselves on the dance floor. I was happy. Suddenly, I couldn't breathe. I needed some air. My heart was palpitating. I just knew that at any minute, the invisible monster was going to show up at my wedding. I made an excuse that we should start packing our gifts to take to the car. While our family was assisting with the packaging, Tommy and I were preparing to leave. Thank God I was able to avoid the invisible monster spoiling my day. Once I got outside and got some fresh air, I could breathe and relax.

We hadn't planned a lavish honeymoon. We went to Atlantic City for three days. I tried talking Tommy out of going. It's not that I didn't want to go. I didn't want to deal with heart palpitations, sweating, shortness of breath, and nausea like I did the first time he took me to Atlantic City. That had been a miserable two-hour ride. Tommy and I went as a couple with his brother, Jake, and Jake's wife. Sitting in the back seat of the large van gave me some comfort. My stress level was running through the roof, but I could somewhat hide what I was experiencing.

I sat so close to Tommy that it made him uncomfortable. I wanted to tell him I felt like I was having a heart attack. Honestly, I just wanted the ride to be over. At one point, Tommy wanted to know why I was drinking so much water. I don't know why, but drinking water always made me feel a little better. I made up some lie that didn't make any sense. I didn't realize how dizzy I was until I almost fainted getting out of the van. The moment we went inside the casino, Princess grabbed me to keep me from falling and took me back outside to get some air. I was so embarrassed. No one, including Tommy, had a clue about what I had going on. Tommy thought I needed something to eat, but I had just eaten before we left. Anyway, I went with Princess to get something to eat to please him. I couldn't enjoy being in the casino, so I went and sat in the van until everyone was ready to go home.

A lot had changed since the time I went to Atlantic City with Jackson. There were no casinos there then. The first night in the hotel on our honeymoon, I put on one of the sexy lingerie items I had received as a gift at my bridal shower. It was black nylon and trimmed with white lace. When I laid down on the bed beside Tommy, he started touching me all over. I couldn't relax. I resisted his touch. The invisible monster was about to take control and spoil my honeymoon. I couldn't breathe. I felt like I was suffocating. And I just wanted to leave. It was something about being in a small place with the door closed that brought me back to the night I was raped. I wanted to escape. Tommy held me tightly in his arms to console me—he had no clue what was wrong with me. After all, I was now his wife, and I shouldn't act that way. I said, "I don't feel comfortable in this room. Can we please go to another hotel?" The room was dark and dainty. It looked like they built it in the 1800s. We had made a reservation at another hotel, but the clerk had rented our room to someone else. She claimed we missed our check-in time.

We had no other choice but to stay in that dainty hotel because all the hotels were booked for the night. My husband booked another hotel the next morning. Thank God I didn't have to deal with the invisible monster when we changed hotels. Once I calmed down, I enjoyed the next two days we were there. We went for long walks on the boardwalk every day. One day as we were taking a walk, many people congratulated us when they read the print on our T-shirts: JUST MARRIED. JULY 14, 1984. I'd had the T-shirts custom made.

When the honeymoon was over, I could feel myself getting anxious about the train ride back to our apartment. Jake and Princess had taken us to Atlantic City because my husband had car trouble. Riding on the train from Atlantic City was nothing like riding on the train to my hometown. I felt like I was riding on a street bus on the railroad track. The ride back was extremely miserable.

Tommy wanted to continue our honeymoon by going to Florida to meet his family members who couldn't attend the wedding. We still had days left before we were supposed to be back at work. My heart almost fell on the floor when he mentioned flying. I wanted to meet his family, but I knew I couldn't fly on a plane. I was fortunate enough to meet Tommy's mother before she passed away when she visited him in New Jersey before we got married. She seemed to be a lovely lady, but I didn't get a chance to know her. Unfortunately, I didn't have the privilege of meeting his father. He passed away soon after we met.

I'd flown on a plane with my sister when we went on vacation to North Carolina. It was terrifying! I feared being that high in the sky, and I was dealing with the invisible monster. When I noticed the flight attendant was serving drinks, I almost grabbed one out of her hand. That was only the second time I'd had drank wine. I made sure I didn't drink the wine like I did before for my low blood pressure. I was totally out of control. I was hoping the wine would calm me down, but it did not. I thought I would pass out when I got off the plane. I was dizzy and could barely stand up. My sister was joking when she said, "You are drunk from all that wine."

The closest airport to my husband's hometown was in Jacksonville, Florida. From there, my husband rented a car to drive to Tallahassee. As I'd anticipated, the two-hour ride in the car was just as miserable as flying on the plane. When Tommy noticed I was acting the same way riding in the car, he became confused. I'd led Tommy to believe I was acting that way on the plane because I feared flying.

Why don't you just tell him how you are feeling? He'll understand. A voice in my head told me to wait but to tell him before we returned home. I prayed I could avoid the invisible monster during my stay in Florida. I was thankful I could relax and have some fun. Once we got settled, I knew it was the perfect time to tell my husband. But I just could not get the nerve to tell him I was insane. I suffered going to and from Florida. When we got back to New Jersey, I sighed with relief.

I often wished I had a solution to my problem. I wanted to explain to my husband the real deal. I continued praying that I would override that monster weighing on my shoulder and that Tommy would know how to handle the truth one day.

When She was Born. My Daughter, Dee

I always said my daughter, Dee, was probably conceived on our honeymoon. Two months after we were married, I discovered I was pregnant, and my due date was May 8, 1985. Predicting labor was hard for doctors to do then, but the nurse got it right that time. I had one child. I named her Dee after a celebrity I watched on a TV show years ago. She was my miracle child. The doctor had predicted I would not carry her to full term because he diagnosed me with fibroids.

Church members, friends, family, and I prayed for a miracle. God answered our prayers. When I changed from a male doctor to a female doctor, she gave me hope. I had no complications. I was in labor for about three hours. My husband was more nervous than me. He was proud to be a father. He celebrated our daughter's birth by buying pink cigars to share with his friends and coworkers.

Tommy wanted me to drive our baby to daycare and not take her on the bus. Every time I practiced driving with my husband, we fought. We were getting nowhere. Tommy decided it was better if I drove alone. It was less of a headache for both of us. I was so nervous the first day I drove to work after my maternity leave ended. My whole body was shaking. I made sure I drove under the speed limit. That made the drivers behind me angry. Often, the drivers would pass me if I was driving on a two-lane street, or the drivers would blow their horns so I would speed up. I was glad when Tommy traded his Buick for a green Ford Tempo. It was much smaller. I had no problem seeing over the steering wheel. I tried to come up with any excuse that would make sense not to drive. Although I told Tommy I didn't feel comfortable driving, he was very persistent. He said the only way I would learn how to drive was to do it alone.

I worried that the invisible monster would interfere with me driving the car. After all, I had trouble riding in one. Although I was nervous when I took driving lessons, I'd hoped learning to drive might be the thing that would finally help me avoid this monster. If I was in control, maybe I wouldn't feel as anxious. Unfortunately, it seemed that I had more fear of driving than riding in a car. I remember driving my sister's new yellow Thunderbird soon after I got my license. As I was making a left turn, the driver behind me almost rammed into me. I was turning too slowly. That made me and my sister so nervous that I didn't drive my sister's car anymore.

The daycare center was just three blocks from where I lived. I wanted my daughter to attend a daycare near where I lived so I didn't have to drive a long distance in heavy traffic. After my daughter had been at the daycare for about three months, things changed. The daycare had to be renovated. I did not like that my daughter was in a large room with children of all ages. I felt she was not getting the care she needed. When I picked her up one afternoon, I noticed the sheet in her crib needed to be changed. She was still lying in vomit from the milk she drank during the day. I was very upset. When I talked to the teacher and asked why the bed had not been changed, she put the blame on another teacher.

So, my husband and I felt it was best to put her in another daycare. When I told my assistant boss, Ms. Harris, how unhappy I was with the daycare, she told me about Babyland Daycare, where her daughter was taking her grandson. Babyland accepted my daughter right away. I was so happy when I changed to the new daycare. It was affiliated with a Catholic church that was across the street from the daycare. It was much nicer, but more expensive. However, it was a load off my shoulders because I didn't have to drive her there. The daycare provided transportation. It was a relief knowing that I didn't have to worry about the invisible monster attacking me with my daughter in the car. The bus driver made sure he arrived on time before I left for work and returned a reasonable time after I got home.

My sister had been living in her new apartment for over a year when she told me the couple that owned the house next door to her was looking for someone nice to rent their second-floor apartment. It was perfect timing. I'd just had my daughter, and we needed the extra bedroom. My husband and I liked the area and the apartment. But I didn't realize how small the living room was in the new place until after we moved in our furniture. I was miserable sitting in that tiny living room on family night when we watched our favorite TV shows. The cramped space was the ideal setting to increase my anxiety to thinking I was suffocating! I never mentioned to my husband how uncomfortable I was. I pretended to enjoy our time together, but secretly, I wanted to move the TV into our bedroom. However, the TV didn't fit. Our daughter's crib took up too much space. Also, my husband didn't like watching TV in bed. I bought another TV and put it in my daughter's room because it was spacious. My daughter's room was where I watched TV. I taped my favorite shows while I was at work and watched them mainly on the weekends.

I liked living in Irvington. It had a lower crime rate than East Orange and Newark. Irvington had been predominately white when I first moved to New Jersey. Still, when Black people started moving there, most white people moved away to other towns. My landlords, Maggie, and her husband Bill, were white. Her son-in-law's father was the mayor. He made sure the police kept our street safe day and night.

When my daughter turned six years old and started kindergarten, I looked forward to taking her to and from school every day. It was about three blocks from where we lived. I decided to explain to my daughter when she would be fully equipped to understand these strange episodes of extreme fear appearing without warning. I felt if she was young, she wouldn't understand. She would have thought I was insane.

I remember when I went on a trip with her kindergarten class to the Staten Island Zoo. On the way there, she didn't have a clue what I was experiencing riding the bus. I started pacing back and forth, trying not to let my daughter see the fear of discomfort I was experiencing. I was in the mode of a fight-or-flight response, trying to counteract the intense feeling of losing control of my body. Fortunately, Staten Island was not a long ride from Irvington.

I couldn't tell my daughter the real reason I didn't want to take her, and her father couldn't take her because he had to work. He couldn't take the day off as I could. I thought about asking my friend Lucy to take her for me, but I couldn't tell her my secret. I knew if I didn't go, my daughter would be the only student in the class that didn't go on the trip.

No way could I have broken her heart. It was an enjoyable trip for the kids. I just pretended to be having as much fun as my daughter while I was freaking out inside.

I suffered again when I went with her to see a football game in Teaneck, NJ, sponsored by our church youth ministry. Although I said I would never go on a church trip again, I felt it was necessary to be with her. She was in the youth choir and all the youth parents planned to go. I didn't want my daughter left behind, even though I knew it was going to be an unpleasant ride for almost thirty minutes. It was like having a nightmare with my eyes open before we got to the football game. On the way there, no one could tell how much I was suffering. I sat in the back with my daughter. She was having so much fun with the kids that she ignored me.

I was miserable. On the ride back, I sat across from Leslie, one of the trip's sponsors. As she talked to me, she noticed how uncomfortable I was. She asked, "Are you okay?" I said I had to go to the bathroom, which was partially true. She said, "Me too! I got to go to the bathroom bad!" That was a good excuse. I couldn't tell her my secret. I wanted to be like everyone else, enjoying the trip. So many times, I tried holding a conversation with Leslie to avoid being so miserable. Occasionally, I glanced at my watch to see how much longer I had to ride. I was so happy when the trip ended. I hadn't lied about having to go to the bathroom because when Leslie dropped my daughter and me off at my apartment, it was the first thing she and I did. We rushed to the bathroom. I could cover up my secret.

I never wanted to deprive my daughter of going on trips, no matter how hard it was for me to ride the bus. When Ms. Greene left the Housing Authority, Ms. Harris was promoted to take her position. There were rumors going around the office that she had been fired. She abruptly left without any explanation. Everyone in the office was so relieved. I enjoyed working with Ms. Harris much better. There was less stress. Ms. Harris oversaw taking the kids in the projects to see a Broadway play in New York. When she offered free tickets for my daughter and me to see the play, I didn't tell her about my experience riding on the bus; I accepted the tickets. She wanted my daughter to go because she'd taken her grandson, who was around her age. I would have liked seeing the show more if Ms. Harris had had enough tickets for my husband. I probably would have felt better.

Just like I'd expected, the invisible monster traveled with us there and back. Particularly on the ride back from New York. This episode of intense anxiety of fear was more severe because the bus suddenly stopped in the middle of the highway. The bus couldn't get enough speed to go up the bridge. It was a school bus, which caused some problems. It wasn't equipped to handle going up a bridge that high. When I realized what was happening, I was so frightened. The bus had stopped high up on the bridge, and fear propelled me. The invisible was attacking my body. It felt like a choking sensation around my neck. I needed air. I couldn't breathe. The kids were having so much fun. Little did they know we were in danger. Traffic was heavy. Any minute, a vehicle could have collided with the bus. I was praying and being attacked by the invisible monster at the same time. It felt like hours before the bus driver could get the bus to start.

As I was getting off the bus, the driver said he could see how afraid I was. I'd been praying, and he knew it. In addition to praying, the invisible monster was taking control. I felt like I was choking, and I couldn't breathe. I was praying to God to please let the bus start because we were in danger. We had no way of contacting anyone to come help us. Back then, cell phones did not exist.

As parents, we do things for our children sometimes just to make them happy. That is why I went with my daughter on those trips. I didn't want her to suffer because of what I was experiencing. Although my daughter was mature and intelligent for her age, I didn't want to put that burden on her shoulders when she was so young. She probably could have accepted it. Most of the time, she let nothing bother her. She is still that way today. At four years old, my daughter knew how to use the phone, write her name, and count to one hundred. In case of an emergency, she needed to know the phone numbers of where my husband and I worked. As soon as she began talking, I taught her the name of our street and the address where we lived.

I was proud of my daughter the day my husband had a seizure when she was home alone with him while I was at work. She was only four years old. Thank God my daughter was aware of my husband having a seizure disorder. I had taught her how to dial my number at work just in case of an emergency. When she called and told me her father was having a seizure, she was calmer than I was. I immediately left my job and went home. In the meantime, I told her to go downstairs to the landlord and have him come upstairs. I instructed her to tell him to press the red button on the medical alert system I had installed that was connected to the hospital system. When my husband had a seizure, all I had to do was press the red button and they would dispatch a paramedic quickly. My daughter followed my instructions. The landlord applauded my daughter for a job well done. He told me my daughter was calm the whole time, and if it were his son, he would have freaked out.

Secrets Revealed

I finally gained enough courage to tell my husband about the night I was raped. I felt it was time for him to know about the traumatic experience I had suppressed for the ten years we had been together. Being in denial that it didn't happen was the best way for me to cope until the day I gave my coworker a ride home from work. We talked about how much we liked *The Oprah Winfrey Show*. When my coworker said some negative things about the sexual assault victims that Oprah had as guests on one of her shows, I disagreed with her. She said, "I didn't believe Oprah and those women when they said they had suppressed the memories of the incident for years. Someone can't forget they had been raped. No woman in their right mind would say something like that." I don't remember if I pushed down harder on the accelerator or pressed on the brake, but I almost snapped because she chuckled as she said those awful things.

It was like a bomb exploded inside me. The tone of my voice was somewhat higher than it usually was when I said, "I believe those women. It is possible to suppress rape because you could be so traumatized you want to believe it never happened." My coworker didn't respond right away when I said, "I know because it happened to me."

Although the rape haunted me, I didn't talk about it until that day. My plan was not to talk about it ever again. But after listening to the ladies on Oprah's show who had been raped, explaining they realized that you are the survivor, and it's not the victim's fault, that was a wake-up call for me. I stop blaming myself. I probably would have never admitted that it was not my fault. Especially after my friend and cousins said, "She should not have done it." I'd never gotten over the fact that Robert was never punished, and I blamed myself.

My coworker was silent for a few minutes. Her voice changed as I told her the story about what had happened to me. She realized it was not a joke. I said, "The entire time he was raping me, other people were standing outside the car watching. I cried and screamed for someone to help me, but no one came to my rescue." I glanced at my coworker while I was telling her about the incident. I could tell she regretted what she'd said.

Although I was upset with my coworker for saying those awful things about the survivors, it gave me the courage to talk about it that night. It was an enormous relief to know I was not alone.

When I talked to my husband about that dreadful night, Tommy understood why I acted the way I did the first time he invited me to his apartment. He recognized the heavy burden I carried. He was distraught that someone could do something like that. He said, "You see, I am not that kind of guy. I would never do a thing like that to you or anyone." After dating him for a while, I knew he was not that type of person.

Not only was I able to accept that it was not my fault, but I could also talk about the incident with other people. I just wish I could have been more open with my husband and other people about the invisible monster. But that was much more difficult to explain. After all, I still didn't know how to label what I was experiencing. Although I could talk about the night I was raped, the invisible monster continued to haunt me. I believed those attacks were related to that night I was raped—mainly because Robert was never punished. No one should be forced to do anything they are not willing to do. The traumatic experience will haunt you for the rest of your life.

Another Doctor

One day, my husband started having chronic seizures. We had been married for about five years and getting along so well. The significant amount of stress gradually increased. It was challenging for me to take care of my daughter and husband. I had no choice but to seek help.

My doctor referred me to another psychiatrist near where I lived. I could see him as often as I liked because I didn't have to pay out-of-pocket like I did when seeing Dr. Miller. The insurance covered the cost. I had high hopes. On my first visit to see Dr. Atkinson, he didn't invite me to lie down on the sofa; I sat in a chair. Dr. Atkinson was a middle-aged white man with gray hair and a caring personality. I know he did everything in his power to help me. Still, I was looking for a miracle. I wanted someone who could help me get rid of the invisible monster immediately. But that didn't happen.

One day, as I was going into the psychiatrist's office, I saw an employee from my job. I worried that she'd tell my coworkers I was seeing a psychiatrist. Then I thought, *If she tells on me, she will be telling on herself as well!* We said hello to each other but did not have a conversation. I am sure she was just as surprised as I was to see me there. Besides, it was no concern of mine why she was there. I just focused on my problem.

Dr. Atkinson prescribed medications. I took one pill during the day for stress. And a different pill at night to help me sleep. Dr. Atkinson told me to be careful not to take a whole pill at night because I needed to adjust to a lower dose first. He often said, "Make sure you split your night pill in half." The medications he prescribed for me were not a magic cure like I was expecting. But I got some results from the pill I took at night. It worked great for a good night's rest.

I still was not getting any results from the medication when I rode in a car. I was so confused. That's why the day I went to Dr. Atkinson's office, the first thing we talked about was the experience I had driving on the parkway. Dr. Atkinson knew my husband was sick and could not drive. And he knew I had trouble riding in a car. I told him I felt I was forced to drive my husband to his job to fill out a medical form. I tried to get some of his friends and family members to drive him, but no one could take that day off work. My husband's medical forms had to be turned in that day for his disability. I didn't have any other options. I had no choice but to try to take him if we wanted to survive. My income couldn't cover all those bills.

It was at that moment that I had to reveal my secret. I had no choice but to tell my husband the truth about I had breathing problems while riding in a car, bus, and train. I don't know if he fully understood what I was saying. I felt he thought I was just too frightened to drive on the parkway. He said, "You can drive on the parkway. I will help you." He was just as anxious as me to get the medical form to his job in time. Because I was scared to death, I had a little talk with Jesus that He would make it right that I could drive on the parkway. I felt I had to do something. It wasn't an easy drive, but I took him.

That was the longest forty-five-minute drive I had ever experienced. Just as I imagined, I was fearful of driving on the parkway and having to deal with the invisible monster too. When I entered the parkway, I couldn't breathe. My heart was palpitating. I felt myself shaking all over.

I wanted to get off. My husband kept talking to me. Occasionally, he would let me know when to change into another lane. As the cars were merging onto the highway, I would scream, "They're going to run into me!" My husband said, "Just keep driving; those cars are not going to run into you." He assured me that nothing was going to happen to me. He seemed to be calm. I thought I was going to have a heart attack. I was happy when I had to stop at the toll booth to pay my fare. That was the only time I could take a deep breath and try to relax for a few seconds. When I got out of the car, I was still shaking. My husband embraced me in his arms and said I did a good job.

The entire time Tommy was talking to his boss, I sat in the waiting area, praying. I knew I had to drive back home. I just wanted to get it over with. The return trip was just like the way there. My husband talked to me the entire way. When we arrived back at our apartment, I said to my husband, "I will never drive on the parkway again."

After the psychiatrist listened to that story, he said the medication was not for fear of riding in a car. The medication was to help with the stress I was going through with my husband. I believe Dr. Atkinson focused more on the stress of dealing with my husband's disability than on me riding or driving a car.

My husband's health was not getting any better—he never returned to work. The doctor said to him if he did not stop drinking, it would shorten his life. His excess drinking of alcohol had induced epileptic seizures. And his high blood pressure was out of control. My husband was oblivious to what I was saying whenever I begged him to stop drinking. We went to counseling for about three months. That was some release, but my husband was no longer engaged with the process.

When I had done everything that I could to stop my husband from drinking, I had a talk with my pastor. He told me, "Mary, he will not listen to you if he doesn't want to stop drinking. Let it go and let God take care of it for you. I will be praying for you."

My husband just ignored what the doctor had to say. As a result, he was forced to go on permanent disability. He struggled with depression. He was disabled. He no longer had a job after eighteen years of working for the Ford Motor Company. It disappointed me when my husband resigned from doing National Guard duties every month after serving eighteen years. That was something he looked forward to after he was discharged from service in the army. It felt like our lives changed overnight. I had to do all the driving. Thank God, I didn't have to take him on the parkway again. I mostly drove in the city. My husband was still able to move around, but he couldn't drive anymore. He mostly walked everywhere he needed to go—the park, the store. Sometimes he would take our daughter, and I would drive to pick them up.

My husband had a seizure every day. I couldn't cope any longer with being stressed out, so I was forced to go on sick leave for three months. When my job granted me a leave of absence, I decided we should move back home. I never liked living in the big city anyway. I will never regret living in New Jersey because that's where I met my husband and we had a beautiful daughter. Besides, I gained a great deal of experience, which helped me a lot. The people in the North were more advanced in doing certain things than what I was used to in the South. The people I dealt with in the North didn't mind hurting your feelings. They would tell you the truth about yourself in front of your face. Some people I dealt with in the South were too afraid of hurting someone's feelings. So, they just kept their thoughts to themselves, which I thought was a bad thing.

Going Home

I was at church one Sunday having a conversation with Leslie when I told her I was moving back to North Carolina. But I needed someone to drive my husband's car because neither my husband nor I could drive us down south. My cousin, Bob, had someone to take our furniture on his tractor trailer, but I didn't know who I could ask to drive my husband's car. My husband felt that if I couldn't drive on the parkway, I could not drive eight hours home. Although I had talked to my husband about the strange feeling I had riding in a car, it had not resonated with him how much I was suffering. Leslie knew my husband was disabled and couldn't drive. I didn't tell her riding in a car made me feel fearful and was why I needed a driver. A heavy burden lifted off my shoulder when she volunteered to drive to North Carolina. She said it was an excellent opportunity to go to South Carolina to visit her family.

I left New Jersey on my way to North Carolina, riding in the back seat of my husband's gray Cougar he had purchased after he got rid of the Ford Tempo. Suddenly, my body was losing control. Breathing became difficult, and I experienced heart palpitations and nausea—the whole nine yards. The only time I felt relief was when we stopped to use the bathroom. Leslie was driving, and my husband sat in the front seat on the passenger side. I sat in the back to be with our six-year-old daughter. That was a perfect excuse. I knew she didn't have a clue what was going on. She slept most of the way.

There was no looking back. I counted the minutes and hours until we arrived at the bus station in Rocky Mount, North Carolina. That was where my brother David planned to meet us to drive us the rest of the way home. I said goodbye to Leslie as she boarded the bus to South Carolina to her hometown. It was a blessing she wanted to drive free of charge, but my husband gave her money, even though she tried to refuse.

I was not going home just for the July 4th holiday this time. I was going to stay for good. At that moment, it was one of the happiest days of my life, besides the day I got married and the day I had my baby girl.

When I left North Carolina to go to New Jersey on a beautiful fall night in September 1970, I felt things could change for the better. I never thought my life could turn upside down for almost all the twenty-one years I lived in New Jersey. I was looking forward to having more good days than bad. But 90 percent of my time in New Jersey, I lived with a secret. Other challenges I faced were far from carrying a secret for so many years. It wasn't easy pretending I wasn't like everyone else, and inside I was freaking out. I was hoping for a new beginning. I knew it wouldn't be a problem staying with my parents until we purchased our home.

I had to get familiar with my town all over again. A lot had changed. Most of my friends were no longer living there. Many of the older people I knew had passed away. Most of the children I knew who were babies when I'd left had grown up to be young men and women with their own kids.

I vaguely remember when my family moved to Simpson. I was only three years old. My grandfather had purchased land in Simpson when my father was three or four years old, and they were the first Black family to move to Simpson. Some of the Gatlin families said they were the first Black family. I will go by what my father said to me. I appreciated my grandfather working so hard to provide his eight children with land and the ability to own their homes. Although they worked on the white man's farm, they didn't have to work as sharecroppers. He did not want his children to be forced to work in the fields.

When I was a child growing up in Simpson, we were poor. For a long time, we didn't have electricity. We used kerosene lanterns. We had to pump our water or use well water for drinking, taking a bath, and washing our clothes. We didn't have inside bathrooms. We had an outside toilet. We used a wood and coal heater to stay warm and cook our food. In the summer, I would have blisters on the bottom of my feet from walking on the hot, dirty road without shoes. I was grateful the streets had been paved, and the town was incorporated with a mayor and three councils. We never had over five hundred people living there. We were all like one big, happy family.

The same year I moved back home, I was appointed to serve on the Planning Board for what would be almost twenty-four years. When the board members asked me to serve as the chair, I hesitated. They asked me when David Boyd became the mayor. Mayor Boyd had been a great chairperson, just as he was a great mayor. He had a pleasant personality and got along with most of the residents. Although I got along with everyone, I wasn't sure if I wanted to accept that responsibility. I had only been on the board for several years. I told the members I wasn't ready. All the board members insisted that I could do the job. So, I accepted, but I worried if the invisible monster would attack me while chairing a group meeting.

Just like I expected, while I was chairing a meeting one night, the invisible monster attacked me. I was talking to the members when suddenly everything in the room turned dark. I could barely see anyone. I believed my nerves got the best of me. I said to the members, "I am sick. I have to leave." I rushed out of the meeting because I was afraid I might faint. The assistant chairperson took over and continued the meeting. I was embarrassed because I had not revealed my secret to Mayor Boyd or the four Planning Board members. However, that did not stop me from chairing other meetings. I did much better when fewer people were attending. I felt more relaxed.

For a while, I worked at the church daycare center next door to my parents' house. My mother was the one who said I should talk to the pastor about getting a job there because she knew he was looking for employees. However, when I went to apply for a job, the daycare was still under construction.

My past working experiences impressed the pastor, so he hired me on the spot to be the church's administrative secretary. Along with the other employees, I agreed to work without pay until he had successfully completed all requirements to open the daycare. That was the worst decision I could have ever made. I didn't know until later that all the employees were receiving a paycheck except for me. Not only was the pastor not paying me, but I did not work as the administrative secretary as he'd promised. Instead, I was a bus monitor to oversee the kids that rode the church van. I sat behind the kids in the van because that helped decreased some of the fear I was encountering. It was a medium-size van with open space, and that helped with my breathing problems. The church van transported most of the kids from the surrounding areas around Simpson and Greenville. Those kids kept me so busy for about two hours that I didn't have time to worry about having to deal with the invisible monster.

I overheard one employee talking about their paycheck when I got off the van one morning going into the daycare. It was at that moment I realized everyone was getting a paycheck besides me. I didn't know why and the staff didn't know why I wasn't getting a paycheck. I was under the assumption that all the employees were still working without pay. My husband was so angry that he told me to resign immediately. He said, "My wife will not be working for anyone without getting paid. I want you to quit today." I didn't resign that day, but I gave the pastor two weeks' notice when I found out that not only was I not getting paid, but he was going to hire someone else to be the church's administrative secretary. Later, I was told that a member of the church wanted her friend to have the position. I told my husband I was going to show the pastor respect, even though he didn't do it to me. My resigning left him without a bus monitor. The daycare teachers rode the bus with the kids until he got a replacement. The pastor did not want to accept my resignation. But he left me with no other choice.

I worked in the Pitt County schools system as a substitute teacher when I quit the daycare. The pay was nothing like what I had made in New Jersey. But it was just a temporary job until I could find something permanent. I worked there for only about three months. That was not what I was used to, anyway. I enjoyed doing administrative work. Although I enjoyed working with kids, it was tough to keep the students under control. One school where I subbed was a long-distance drive from my house. I didn't know if I could drive that far. Just like I expected, driving was very difficult. I was a nervous wreck when I reached the school. All the way to work, I had heart palpations, dizziness, and nausea.

Being a substitute teacher, you may be called to fill in for any teacher at any school in your area. The overwhelming, extreme tense of driving more than six miles to different places was more than what I could deal with. I knew working in the school system was not for me. I resigned.

I was at my wit's end looking for a job when I went to a temp agency seeking employment. I was not expecting to take a typing test. It amazed the agent how fast I could type. She got me a job at Pitt Memorial Hospital (Vidant) in the records department as a filer the same day. I suppose beggars can't be choosers, but I wanted to do administrative work. I didn't mind filing, but that type of work kept you on your feet most of the day. And the small space I worked in made it feel like I was suffocating.

After working there for about a month, the supervisor said she liked my work and wanted me to go to human resources to apply to become permanent. I was not expecting that in such a short time. Most temporary agencies, you might work a day, week, or however long you are needed. But I never went to human resources because I was miserable. The tight space between the two file cabinets made it difficult for me to breathe. The office was small, and I was not near any windows.

I was experiencing heart palpitations and nausea every day. One day, I was so dizzy that I vomited, and I had to go to the emergency room. It broke the supervisor's heart when I resigned.

When I moved back home, my parents were in their late seventies. All my siblings had moved out and were married. My nephew, Darnell, stayed with them most of the time. But when I moved back home, he was away in college, finishing his last year in law school. My mother was so happy I had moved back. My sister Bell and her husband had moved back from New Jersey two years before me. She was settled with a good job and a nice place to live. Although my mother knew it was difficult for my sister to find a good-paying job in the South, she was happy when we returned home. My parents didn't mind giving up their bedroom for my husband and me. They slept in the guest bedroom. My daughter slept in the bedroom near the kitchen. I was grateful my parents had the house remodeled and had added on an extra bedroom. And I no longer had to use an outside toilet.

I was sitting in my parents' den when suddenly it felt like I was hallucinating. I was breathing fast, and I felt like I needed oxygen. I didn't know how to tell my family what I was experiencing because I had not revealed my secret. The den was one of the smallest rooms in my parents' house, with no windows and only a tiny amount of light. It used to be our kitchen when I was growing up until my father expanded the house to become three bedrooms and added a bath. My parents used the den as a place to relax and watch TV.

Whenever I sat in the den to watch TV or chat with my parents, I lost control. I couldn't breathe. When I needed air, I made some excuse to escape to my bedroom as a cover-up. When I told my husband that I wanted to buy a TV to put in our bedroom, he was okay with it. Although he didn't enjoy having a TV in the bedroom, he knew it was just temporary. Anyway, that was my father's favorite room. He mostly sat in the den watching TV, reading the Bible, and napping.

My husband and daughter really enjoyed living in my hometown. They started making friends right away. They didn't have any problems getting acquainted with the people in the small community. Everybody knew everybody and everybody's business. Tommy liked that when he went places, he no longer had to deal with a crowd of people most of the time. It was essential to both of us that we raise our daughter where the crime rate was low. I appreciated living in a small community/rural area, where the air quality was much better as well.

I started attending my old church. My husband loved going to church. He hardly ever missed a Sunday. My mother was a member for over seventy years.

My brother David was a deacon, and my mother and sister Mae became deaconesses of the church soon after I was reinstated. Most of the members were my former classmates or cousins. After joining, I saw they added two bathrooms: one left of the vestibule, the other on the right. Progress! I was grateful the church had inside toilets. I didn't like using the outside toilet that was near a wooded area. I would always look for any type of insects that might bite me while sitting on a piece of wood that covered the hole in the ground. For wiping, toilet paper was nonexistent. We used newspapers and catalogs.

Although the church now had inside toilets, other areas needed severe repairs. I was so happy that the members were looking for a location to build a new sanctuary. Just like me, most of the members didn't like the location of the church sitting off the highway near a wooded area, especially when we had services at night. It would be pitch dark outside. And during the summer, the members would be afraid of stepping on snakes inside and outside of the church.

My mother wanted me and my family to sit in the front with her. I didn't dare tell her the secret I had been keeping from her for so many years. Even though she saw me with a smile on my face, little did she know I was freaking out inside. I led her to believe that my husband preferred sitting in the back of the church, which was partially true. My mother was a firm believer that if you sat in the back of the church, you had more distractions and might miss a lot of what was going on.

23

Fear of Flying

When I started working temporarily at the hospital and public school, my husband's disability was approved. We purchased a mobile home and placed it on the empty property next to my parents' house at their insistence. My parents insisted we place our mobile home on the empty property next to their house, which was a great idea, as my father was no longer able to cultivate the property. For years, he used that property for vegetable gardening. After my parents died, I became the owner of the property in 2014. After my father's death at 79 in March 1999, my mother owned the property until her death at 98 in June 2014.

After we moved into our new home, I had high hopes that my life would change for the better. When my husband and I became homeowners and the mortgage was in our names, I gained a sense of security and peace of mind. Renting in New Jersey meant we couldn't make changes to the place. I liked my new home because I didn't have to struggle with needing more space. All the rooms were very spacious, so I didn't fear having those strange feelings the way I did in my apartment. When we had family night, I could sit in the den, watch TV, and breathe comfortably.

I was praying my husband's drinking would stop when we moved south. Instead, it became a bigger problem. He drank every day. It was important for Tommy to quit drinking and give up alcohol entirely, per the doctor's orders. Alcohol was the one thing that put a damper on our marriage. I told Tommy the story about the first time I drank wine. He said I was drinking the wrong type of wine, and I should have been drinking a glass of red wine. The only reason I let him encourage me to drink was that I thought it would ease some of those feelings of losing control. Unfortunately, the three years I drank wine didn't help my situation. After I drank wine for a while, I got comfortable drinking around other people. It was no big deal to the people in New Jersey the way it was in my hometown. Most of the people I knew drank anyway.

I only drank socially. I would drink when I went to a function for my job or at one of my husband's family gatherings. If I had a stressful day, I would have a drink at home.

My husband's family drank. Everyone at my job drank like fish. Before I began drinking wine, I felt out of place. Everyone would have a drink in their hand except me. When I realized that drinking was not helping me with my problems, I stopped drinking. I had a daughter, and I didn't want her to see both of her parents drinking. I didn't have a problem if someone wanted to drink alcohol. It just wasn't for me. My husband, however, drank excessively. It was causing him to have more seizures. His alcoholism was affecting our marriage. He could have seizures at any time. It made me nervous when he went out with his drinking buddies.

The paramedics came to our house so often, that's when most people down south learned my husband was a seizure patient. When we lived in New Jersey, I had purchased a necklace for him to wear that would inform people of his illness in case he became nonresponsive. Several months before we moved to the South, he was walking home from the corner grocery store one evening and had a seizure. Right away, they knew he had a medical condition by seeing the necklace. When my husband didn't come home at a reasonable time, I walked around the apartment on eggshells. It was around midnight when the hospital called to say an ambulance had taken him there. I don't know why it took the hospital so long to call me.

When people drink as he did, it caused them to have many problems, physically and emotionally.

What freaked me out was when my sister-in-law called to tell me my husband became ill while visiting his family in Florida. She said he was in the hospital and was semi-comatose. I told my sister-in-law Mattie that the only way to get there quickly was to take a plane. By then, Tallahassee had an airport, and I didn't have to take the plane to Jacksonville like before. On the ride to the airport, I was worried about my husband and about having to deal with the invisible monster. I didn't want to fly on the plane because of my past experiences. But I had no other choice. I just said a prayer. *Lord, please help me take this trip.*

As I was boarding the plane, I wanted to sit in the back. But the flight attendant directed me to sit over the wing. I became even more fearful when the flight attendant said I was responsible for making everyone safe if something went wrong with the plane. I thought, *I am the wrong person for this responsibility.* The plane was full, so I had no other choice but to sit there. I twisted and turned for two hours, trying to counteract my strange reactions until I got off the plane.

Thank God when Mattie picked me up from the airport and took me to the hospital to visit my husband, he was no longer semi-comatose. My husband was still weak, but the minute I walked into the room to see him, he perked up with a big smile on his face. I spent the first night with him and visited every day until he was well enough to be discharged from the hospital. I didn't dare tell him how fearful I was when flying back home alone. I went back home before my husband so I could take care of our daughter, and he flew back several days later. He stayed the extra time with his family to make up for the days he missed of his visit while he was in the hospital.

I was freaking out flying back alone. I felt like I was having a heart attack when I had to change planes when I arrived in North Carolina. The second plane was smaller. I experienced a fight-or-flight response when I was again assigned to sit over the wing. The passenger across from me noticed I was so afraid. He assured me that a small plane was safer. He said, "Did you know sitting over the wing, you have a better chance of surviving?" I nodded and smiled. Little did he know I was more fearful of the invisible monster attacking me than I was sitting over the wing! I dared not tell him what I was experiencing. I just led the passenger to believe I was fearful of flying.

Saying Goodbye

My husband continued doing what the doctors in North Carolina and New Jersey had warned him not to do. Drinking a lot caused my husband to have multiple seizures. I constantly had to call the rescue squad to take him to the hospital. My husband died October 3, 1994, five years before my father's death. The night my husband died, a part of me went with him. I thought I was going to pass out or have a heart attack, just like my husband. Thank God we lived behind my parents. My parents and my siblings were there for my daughter and me. My parents were just as distraught and emotional about my husband's death as my daughter and I were.

I asked my husband countless times to stop drinking, but so many people told me: "You are not the one to stop a person from drinking. That is something they have to decide for themselves." Our married life would have been almost perfect if he'd not had a problem with alcohol. So many people loved him. Losing a partner is something you will never get over. I will miss him until the day I die.

Every night for about three weeks, my parents stayed with my daughter and me until I was strong enough to stay alone. My daughter was nine years old when her father died. She went into denial right away. It took some time for her to accept that her father was gone and never coming back. Some days, she would just cry for him for a long time. They were so close. She is a strong person, so it didn't stop her from excelling in school. I knew her father would have been proud of her for being an *A* student in school and college. In all her activities, he supported her. One Sunday in New Jersey, when she was about six years old, we went to one of her ballet concerts, and my daughter forgot her steps. My husband whistled at me and said with a big smile on his face,

"Look at our daughter. I don't think she knows that all the other kids are dancing the same way except her." My daughter soon realized she was out of line and cried. My husband was about to get her off stage. I begged him not to.

When we moved to the South, she was in another ballet class. I think that incident in New Jersey stuck with her. She was one of the best ballet dancers in the class. Every year, the ballet school would have a dance recital for all the kids. Her first recital was the last time her father went to one of her activities before he passed away.

25
Michael

My sister Mae was right when she said I could probably get a job through the Human Resource Development program offered at Pitt Community College. So, I joined the program. I was desperately in need of a job, or I'd be running out of money soon. A couple of weeks before the program ended, the instructor had the students go on job interviews. I went to Greenville Housing Authority because of my previous working experience at Newark Housing Authority.

To my surprise, when I walked into the office, I heard someone say, "Hi, Mary." At first, I didn't recognize Pamela. After all, it had been years since I had seen her. She and I attended Pitt Community College during the time I attended with John, Bill, and Carolyn. Pamela had been working at the Housing Authority for years in the Finance Department. I was so happy she was part of the interview.

Four or five people interviewed me, and it went well. The executive director, Mr. Brown, resembled my former boss: white, tall, with sandy hair, and around fifty years old. I liked him immediately.

A couple of days later, Pamela called to tell me I had gotten the job. I can't tell you how excited I was landing a job doing similar work to what I had done at the Newark Housing Authority for sixteen years. The federal government funds public housing, and I knew how the system worked.

For a while, I worked on a grant for the self-sufficiency program for tenants living in the projects. I knew the job would only be temporary if the grant wasn't approved. Most of the tenants didn't have confidence that the program would be a success. According to them, this was not the first time the housing authority had applied for a grant, and nothing happened. I needed a job, so I took a chance and crossed my fingers that the grant would be approved. Mr. Brown hired only three people to do the job. Dr. Barnes was the supervisor, as he had a great deal of experience completing grant applications. Also, he was a full-time professor at East Carolina University (ECU). Betty, a beautiful, young white girl, was the third person hired. She was in her late twenties, much younger than me. We worked well together. Some days, Dr. Barnes came to the office just long enough to give Betty and me our assignments. The rest of the day, he would be at ECU. Of course, we could call him if we had questions. The tenants were excited the Housing Authority was working on a grant to help them become self-sufficient. The work was easy, the pay was good, and I enjoyed working in the office. It was a nice size, and there weren't many people crowding me.

Michael was hired as a computer repairman. He liked being around me more than the other girls. I felt like his little sister when I stood beside him because he was about six feet tall. I didn't realize that he wanted a relationship until my boss told me one day how much Michael liked me. I nipped it in the bud because I wanted a friendship, not a relationship. I was in my late forties, and I think he was in his late thirties. I did not want to be a cougar. My husband had just recently passed away, and all my focus was on my daughter. Occasionally, I went out with him to different functions as a friend, but we never went out as a couple.

All the employees liked Michael. He was a whiz on the computer. Whenever there was a problem, Michael could fix it. Michael was a big help to me when I became the church clerk. He showed me and some members at church how to use QuickBooks. It was a relatively new program that helped track your finances. Michael and I worked diligently, spending endless nights working with QuickBooks to get the church finances in order. Although I was appointed to be the church clerk, I continued working with the financial secretary until I resigned.

When Michael found out my nephew invited me to his graduation from law school, he volunteered to take my daughter and me. I wanted to say no because I knew it was going to be a long and miserable ride. The only reason I went was because I felt guilty I didn't attend my niece Louise's graduation. The ride to her graduation at UNC-Chapel Hill was a slightly longer ride than to Durham, NC. I had the same problem when my sister Mae graduated from Mount Olive College. It was less than an hour's ride. But it didn't matter how long the ride was. It still was a problem. I just couldn't get enough courage to tell my niece or sister why I couldn't attend their graduations. I made up a lame excuse and sent my sister flowers, and I gave Louise money as a gift.

When I rode to Durham in Michael's white SUV on the way to my nephew Darnell's graduation, it was like living in a nightmare for two and a half hours. I thought I was going to die. Occasionally, I drank water and fumbled in my pocketbook, hoping that would help take my mind off what I was experiencing. But no matter how much I tried talking to Michael and my daughter, it didn't remove the fear.

Thank God I didn't suffer during my nephew's graduation ceremony. I thought everything was going well until we went to the restaurant where we celebrated with him. I didn't know the celebration was going to happen. I said, "I don't think we should go. Don't you guys see it's about to storm?" Of course, they ignored me and went anyway. I tried to come up with every excuse in the book not to go, but no one listened to me. I went knowing I didn't want to be caught in a severe storm and having a sudden episode of intense fear from riding in the car at the same time.

Thank God the ride to the restaurant was short because soon after we got on the highway, the storm was in full force. The wind was very high, and torrents of rain were coming down. Michael and my daughter thought it was the destructive storm that was frightening me. We arrived at the restaurant safe and sound. Some people in the restaurant said we had gone through a tornado. That was the last thing my family wanted to hear. I said to them, "You should have listened to me in the first place." I was a nervous wreck. And I believe they were too.

The last time I remember going out with Michael was when he took my daughter and me to Busch Gardens Amusement Park in Virginia. I dreaded going. But I wanted my daughter to go someplace other than church and school. Most of her friends had gone and told her about so many exciting things to do at Busch Gardens. I just couldn't say no. On the way there, I thought I would die when Michael drove across a long bridge. I couldn't breathe. I just knew it was my last day on earth. My heart was thumping like a drum. So many times, I wanted to tell Michael to please stop the car, but I knew that wasn't possible. I am sure he grew tired of me asking him so many times how much longer before we would get off the bridge. If only I dared to tell him my secret, I believe he would have understood. But I didn't want to be labeled crazy. He couldn't help me. At that point in my life, no one could help me.

When we finally got off the bridge and arrived at Busch Gardens, I felt like doing a happy dance. It took me a while to compose myself while we were walking around the park. We spent most of the day there. I liked that my daughter was having so much fun. She and Michael rode some rides while I watched. I dared not ride on anything. I did not want my daughter or Michael to see me having these strange reactions I couldn't explain. As well as thinking I was crazy. I almost didn't want the day to end and dreaded the ride back. When Michael said he wanted to take my daughter shopping and to get something to eat in another town before we went home, I wanted to scream. I just wanted to get the long ride back home over with. While shopping and eating at the restaurant, I focused my mind on the long ride back. It was like he was reading my mind when he took another route back instead of going across that long bridge. It was not as bad as it had been riding on that long bridge.

Mr. Brown called me into his office one day and said, "Mary, you know the grant didn't go through. I am going to have to close the office." At that moment, all I could think about was the hard work Dr. Barnes, Betty, and I had put into the grant proposal. We couldn't believe it had been rejected. He was supposed to be a whiz with getting grant proposals approved. If we didn't get approved, we would have no jobs. Not only were we upset, but so were the residents who were looking forward to achieving self-sufficiency. Not in a million years could we have predicted there would be a large earthquake when we submitted the grant proposal. When the earthquake came to California, a portion of the grant money we were competing for went toward the damages. And the rest went to public housing, which came in first place.

...

Mr. Brown said to Betty and me, "You guys did a good job, but not good enough." I knew he was serious by the look on his face. "We came in third place." Mr. Brown was a person who said what was on his mind. He didn't sugarcoat anything. We knew that was the end of the road for us. Betty and I continued going to work for a while, doing absolutely nothing. Luckily, Mr. Brown needed a receptionist to work in Section 8. He said, "Mary, I regret I have to let you go because I know you need a job to take care of your daughter. I know you need the money, so I would like to offer you the receptionist's job." At that moment, I wanted to jump up and hug his neck. I couldn't thank him enough. I had a permanent job with benefits. I had never worked in the Section 8 department before. Still, I knew it was a voucher program that assisted very low-income families. Working there was like a dream come true.

When my new supervisor Elaine showed me where I would sit in the receptionist area, I feared of having reoccurring visits from the invisible monster in that small and tight space. I thought, *I need this job. I will not let this monster take control of me*. It eased my mind to realize there were two doors to enter the receptionist's area. That helped me avoid the feelings of suffocation. I never kept both doors closed at the same time. I liked the idea that I could get some fresh air when I walked outside to the primary office throughout the day to take mail or send a fax. There was no doubt in my mind that I could handle the work because it was easy and by far the least stressful job I ever had.

The Monster Revealed

I worked at the Greenville Housing Authority for about four years before the invisible monster attacked me at work. It took me entirely by surprise. Although I still had an intense fear of riding or driving in a car, I drove six or seven miles every day to work with no issues. And I hadn't had any problems at work, either. But when I walked into the receptionist area to sit down after lunch, I noticed I wasn't feeling well. I had this loud ringing in my left ear, which felt like it was going to explode. I was overwhelmed with fear when suddenly I felt dizzy and nauseous. I could feel my heart beating fast, and I couldn't breathe. I was familiar with the abrupt feeling of intense fear and extreme nervousness. Still, I didn't know what was causing the loud hissing sound in both of my ears. When I got control of myself, I took a walk to the kitchen area to buy a soda out of the machine to ease my nausea. Unfortunately, that made me feel worse. I was so scared; I did not know what to do. I made an appointment to see my doctor right away.

Dr. Watkins was my primary doctor when I moved back to North Carolina. He was booked that day, so I couldn't see him. The nurse practitioner saw me instead. After she examined my ears, she said, "I think you have vertigo."

"What is that?" I had never heard of it before. I was in my early fifties when I had my first vertigo attack. I had never had a problem with having vertigo or the hissing sounds in my ear. It didn't take long for me to understand after she explained it to me. This was the beginning of me having to deal with having vertigo for a long time. It's not a good feeling being dizzy and nauseous just about every day, and most significantly, the hissing sound in my ears. That drove me crazy. I didn't know vertigo could trigger some of the unexplained feelings I were experiencing. I just wanted the loud hissing sound in my ears to stop. She treated me for that.

I carried my secret for over twenty years before I finally revealed to my family what I was experiencing. About a week after that first attack at work, I had to walk outside to go to the main office to take mail and send a fax. On my way back to my office, I felt the scorching sun beaming down on my head—the temperature had to have been around 100 degrees. I felt like I was going to melt. I was walking fast to get back into my office to cool off under the air conditioner. Once inside, I pulled my chair away from my desk to sit down, when suddenly the room went dark, and my head was spinning like a top. My heart was palpitating so fast that it felt like I was having a heart attack. I couldn't see. I was scared, and I needed air. I thought I was dying. I could no longer hold back from telling my coworkers what felt like a life and death situation I was experiencing. I screamed. Everyone in the office came running into the reception area. My coworkers were in shock. Judy and Amy were Section 8 representatives. I took most of their calls. Judy's office was across the walkway from where I sat. I believe Judy was the first one in my office. She said, "What's wrong?"

I kept saying, "I can't see. I can't breathe. I don't feel good." I just knew I was dying. Judy was so afraid. She called 911. I didn't learn until later that I had scared Judy so bad, she dialed 411 instead of 911. Amy's office was one door down from Judy. When she saw how hysterical Judy was, she had to dial 911 for her. By the time the paramedics came, I was coming around somewhat. The paramedics thought I had gotten too hot because they had taken many people to the hospital that day for the same reason.

Someone in the office called my sister Mae, who was at work, to let her know what happened. She worked about two blocks away from me. Mae got in touch with my parents and the rest of my family. It was a good thing they all were there at the hospital when I told them my secret. I had no other choice. My parents, along with my two sisters, were listening to the physician when he said I had vertigo, and it had triggered me into having a panic attack.

That's when I said, "So, you mean to tell me when I felt like my body was losing control, what I have been having for so long were panic attacks?" I said I didn't tell anyone because I thought I was crazy. That was the first time I heard the term "panic attack." I had no clue what it was. The doctor assured me I was not crazy, and he gave me information to read about panic attacks. It was like I had been born again to know that I was not crazy. I kept repeating to myself, T*hank God, I am not crazy*. Although the doctor couldn't tell me the reason for all the other panic attacks I had experienced, he told me that the panic attack I'd had that day was related to vertigo.

I researched panic attacks on the Internet, gathering more information so I could fully understand what I was experiencing. When I had my first panic attack, it was in the 1970s, and there was no clear information about the illness. Doctors began recognizing panic attacks in the early 1980s. Although I had panic attacks in the 1980s, I'm not sure my doctors would have been able to diagnose my problem even if I had told them about my situation. When I explained to the two psychiatrists about the unexpected and intense feelings I was experiencing, they didn't diagnose me with having panic attacks. I was treated for stress anxiety related to panic attacks, but it didn't explain why. I only wished I'd known sooner how to label what I was experiencing. I could have gotten some help much earlier. I blame myself for not telling the truth. But the one thing I recognized was that it was a mental health problem. And I knew I needed psychiatric help.

My family was in a state of shock that I'd carried that secret from 1975 until 1999. I said to my family, "I was afraid to tell anyone. I didn't know what it was. I didn't want to be labeled as a crazy person." Looking back, I knew that if only I had understood panic attacks, my parents would have understood too. I was glad my father learned about panic attack disorder before he passed away. I appreciate that he stood by me whenever I needed him. I had a good father and mother.

It was a relief that I could now talk about my secret to my family. It was a load off my shoulders when I told them that the panic attacks were the reason I couldn't ride the bus, in a car, or fly on a plane. My sister Bell understood when I said the panic attacks were why I'd wanted to move out of Mattie's apartment and didn't want to go riding with her when she bought her first car. Mae understood that panic attacks were the reason I hadn't attended her graduation. And my family understood why I didn't go a lot of places with them. Not one time did anyone think I was crazy like I'd expected. I am sure they felt that way because they were learning about my panic attacks in the '90s and not in the '70s when I started having them. I am almost sure I would have been labeled crazy back then, because like me, I didn't know panic attack disorder existed.

The day I went back to work, my coworkers were happy to see that I was doing much better. They'd thought I was dying. When I told my coworkers I'd had full-blown vertigo and a panic attack, I was relieved I could talk about my secret. I no longer feared being labeled as crazy because, by the '90s, most people knew about panic attacks. If I had not been too ashamed to share what I was going through, I would have known what I was experiencing and gotten help sooner.

I withheld my secret from the church members until one Saturday at choir rehearsal. About thirty members were present, and I felt closed in. Suddenly, I felt I couldn't breathe. Before I could go outside to get some fresh air, I became dizzy. I thought I was going to pass out. Everyone was so fearful. My cousin Bob came to my rescue. He worked at the hospital and immediately knew what to do. He pulled out his cell phone and called 911. When the paramedic examined me before taking me to the hospital, I said I had vertigo and panic attacks. Although I was in no danger, they took me to the hospital to get a thorough examination. I already knew they would give me an IV, chest X-ray, and CT scan before they sent me home, even though nothing was physically wrong. Later, the members learned I have panic attack disorder. Most of them knew about panic attacks. But some didn't have a clue what it was. I wish I could have been as strong as my cousin Carol when she'd had her first panic attack while driving her car. She said, "Girl! I didn't let it take control of me. I tried to stay calm. I talked myself out of it. And I never had one since." That was one thing I later learned; it is essential not to let the fear of a panic attack control you. You must manage it before it goes out of control.

I had another panic attack at a restaurant when my sister and I went to lunch together. That was the end of the road for me. It had been sweltering outside. As my sister and I were waiting for about five or ten minutes to be served, I noticed how crowded it was. The restaurant was small and tight. I said to Mae, "I don't feel well." My head was spinning. I was so dizzy that I couldn't see. I was having heart palpitations, and I was petrified. I needed air. Mae was also terrified. That was her first time seeing me in that condition. But thank God she knew about my secret, and she knew what to do. She went to get help right away, and someone in the restaurant called the paramedics. They took me to the hospital for the third time and diagnosed me with the same problem. My heartbeat was normal. I had no breathing problems. I'd just had a vertigo attack, along with a panic attack. After the episode at the restaurant, I had to go on medical leave for a month.

When I went to see the nurse practitioner for a follow-up ordered by the physician at the hospital, I didn't have to hold back my secret anymore. I told her about the panic attack episode along with the vertigo attack. I had no fear of telling her how long I'd had panic attacks. She didn't think I was crazy, nor was she surprised. She said, "Many people have panic attacks. Just recently, they came out with a new medication I think will help you." She prescribed Paxil. That was good news to my ear. *I can finally overcome losing control of my body and won't have any more panic attacks.*

But the first time I took the medication, I was disappointed to find it wasn't working. It seemed to trigger a panic attack. The pill was too strong for my body. I didn't know if it was because I was underweight and I needed a lower dose, but the medication caused me to experience hallucinations. I immediately called the nurse practitioner. I said, "I can't take this medication. I think it's too strong. Every time I take a pill, I have trouble breathing."

She said, "You need to continue taking the pills until your body adjusts to the medication. Once you take the Paxil, you have to finish taking all of them." I couldn't deal with the miserable feeling. I discontinued the medication.

When Dr. Watkins had an opening, I went to see him. I said, "I stopped taking the Paxil that your nurse practitioner prescribed. I was having side effects. I think the medication is too strong." Dr. Watkins took me off the medication. He said, "Since you can't take any medication, I'm going to refer you to see a physical therapist for your vertigo and panic attacks."

I'd had so many panic attacks, I had to stop driving. My daughter was seventeen. Thank God she had taken driver's education and gotten her license when she turned sixteen. She took me to my appointments before she went to college. I felt she was old enough to understand what I was experiencing. I noticed that every time my daughter took me for a visit, she would ask the physical therapist many questions. And she paid close attention to the exercises the physical therapist had me do. Most of the exercises were walking around inside the building and distinct movements with my eyes. My daughter was so impressed that it prompted her to become a physical therapist because she wanted to learn more about panic attack disorders to help me.

It was difficult for me to accept my panic attacks were getting worse, and I could no longer keep them a secret from my boss and coworkers. I had no clue why the doctor at the hospital didn't refer me to see a psychologist after he diagnosed me with panic attacks. I thought the medication I was taking for vertigo would help me. What was so debilitating for me was that once I had a panic attack at work, I feared it would happen again. I did not want my boss and coworkers to deal with those episodes of panic every day. I felt like the invisible monster had defeated me. He'd won. I realized I could no longer cope with having a panic attack at work every day. When my medical leave was up, I could not return to work. So, I applied for permanent disability. I had no other choice but to resign. My plan had been to work until I was at retirement age. When I quit working at fifty-five, it was a hard pill to swallow. Also, it was hard saying goodbye to my coworkers the day I cleaned out my desk and gave Elaine my resignation. I held back the tears.

...

I was sitting at the kitchen table when suddenly I had a panic attack. It was like the one I had at work in my office that day. No matter how many times I had a panic attack, they terrified me. The paramedics took me to the hospital by ambulance for the fourth time.

My mother was in the kitchen washing her dishes when she looked out the window and saw the paramedics going into my house. When she realized I'd had a panic attack, she calmed down. My mother and father followed the paramedics to the hospital in my father's car. It embarrassed me watching the neighbors standing outside when they put me inside the ambulance. I don't know what my mother said to them when the neighbors asked what was wrong. At first, they thought the paramedics were there for one of my parents. The doctors and nurses knew me already because I had been to the hospital so many times for the same things. No matter how many times I survived a panic attack, I would go to the hospital because I still wasn't fully educated on how to handle a panic attack or vertigo. I couldn't take medication to help me.

When the nurse with an African accent came into the room and read my chart, she looked at me with a smile. She kindly said, "When you feel a panic attack about to come, don't fight it. Just let it happen." She said that I could avoid coming to the hospital so often if I didn't fight the fear of an attack. I knew that was excellent advice, but it was difficult for me to sit there and let it happen. I felt God was telling me the same thing that day as I was praying to Him to please help me. At that moment, it was like a soft voice whispering in my ear to repeat every day: "I did not give you the spirit of fear, but of power, love, and a sound mind." Unfortunately, I repeated that scripture only about three or four times. Whenever I had an attack, my fear caused me to forget to repeat the scripture. However, that scripture became significant and valuable to me one day.

I said to Dr. Watkins, "I am embarrassed going to the hospital for the same thing all the time. I don't enjoy having panic attacks in front of people. I can't take it anymore." I was going through hell.

Dr. Watkins said, "Your body rejected the medication. Your insurance will no longer cover visits to a physical therapist. I'm going to refer you to see a psychiatrist to help with the panic attacks." I said I had seen two psychiatrists already, and neither could help me.

Dr. Watkins said, "I think this psychiatrist can help you. Just make an appointment to see her." I knew Dr. Watkins was trying to help me. My life was in a twilight zone. I needed help. So, I made an appointment to see the psychiatrist he recommended.

Although I had doubts, I felt comfortable going to Dr. Strong's office because she was a middle-aged white woman and owned a private practice. I felt more comfortable in that setting than in the other two psychiatrists' offices I went to in the past. Dr. Strong hesitated about prescribing any type of medication when I explained my reaction to Paxil. Instead, she had me see a therapist who worked under her.

The first therapist I went to see was a young white man who was still in training at East Carolina University. I don't remember his name because I saw him only about three times. After him, I saw and liked Ms. Anderson right away.

For about two years, I went to see Ms. Anderson. She had retired after working at the hospital for a long time and was working part time for Dr. Strong. I admired she could still drive in her early eighties and work part time. My sessions with Ms. Anderson lasted an hour. When she said the cost would be $90.00 each visit, I was afraid my insurance wouldn't cover it. I suppose mental health was different because it covered me 100 percent.

During my first session with Ms. Anderson, she was aware I couldn't take any medications. She told me that without medication, it would take longer for me to get results. Ms. Anderson asked me a lot of questions about my childhood and my family life. I was glad I could open up to her about being raped and about the first time I had a panic attack. It was a relief to talk about my problem.

After I had gone to Ms. Anderson for a while, she said I was afraid of my past. I was holding on to things I needed to let go of. I had never let go of the night Robert raped me. Although I could talk about that night, I needed closure. I'd never gotten over the fact that Robert was not punished for what he did to me. Also, I kept my panic attack disorder a secret for over twenty years, preventing me from having a good life.

We talked a lot about my husband, but she never related my problem to my deceased husband. It surprised me when she said the only thing that made me happy was my daughter and family. She said my daughter was a big help in my life. I never realized that my strength was coming from my daughter and my family. Looking back, I trusted no one. After the rape, it took a long time before I could trust a man. My husband was the only man I dated that I felt the most comfortable being with. It's not that I didn't have love for everyone, but sometimes the faith you put in a person can end up disappointing you. That happened to me with my girlfriend's sister when Robert raped me, and again, in my early twenties with one of my girlfriends, who I thought would never hurt me, did. When she spread a lie about me to the people in the community, it led me not to trust women for a long time.

Ms. Anderson did everything she could, trying to help me let go of the past and deal with what was happening in the present. Her primary concern was for me to concentrate on raising my daughter. I felt I was making some progress with Ms. Anderson, just talking to her for an hour. She was the only person who seemed to understand my problems. Unfortunately, it didn't take away the panic attacks. If she had not died before my sessions ended, I believe I would have overcome having panic attacks with or without medication. I made some progress just talking to her. The conversations we had made me realize how I needed to face my fear of being raped, stress, and panic attacks.

I made a conscious decision not to see another psychiatrist after Ms. Anderson passed away because it had been years and lots of frustration trying to get a proper diagnosis. Although I had no plan of my own to cope with the panic attacks, I felt like you could stick a fork in me because I was done. I was convinced that the more I prayed, the worse I was getting. It was like my prayers were hitting the ceiling and bouncing back on me without an answer. But I never gave up on God.

I was getting lonely and depressed when I could no longer drive or go anywhere besides church. I had no clue how long it would be before I could drive again.

My brother knew how important it was for my mother and me to attend church services. So, he drove out of his way just to take us to church after my daughter left for college. She'd been my driver. Every time I drove my car, I became anxious. It was like when I first started driving. I would be fearful and shaking the entire time. I felt out of control and couldn't wait until I got to where I was going so I could calm down. I felt lonely being in the house without my daughter and my husband.

Thank God I did church work at home to keep me motivated. I enjoyed helping the financial secretary and typing the church worship services programs every week. And on some occasions, I typed programs for weddings, funerals, and other special occasions for some members for free. I liked I could do my work any time of the day or night. That was something I looked forward to doing every day. After all, I could no longer hold down a regular job, and I didn't have to fear a boss or my coworkers dealing with me having those episodes every day.

27
You Can Do It

When my panic attack disorder was totally out of control, I didn't know what to do. It overwhelmed me that the invisible monster had taken control of my body, mind, and soul. I couldn't drive anymore. My mother and daughter knew I was fighting two hurdles against the monster. He had taken control of me riding in a car, now I couldn't drive a car. It was like my mother and daughter had enough. They were not about to sit back and let the monster stop me from driving a car. They repeatedly told me, "You can do it."

When I got enough courage to drive my car to take my mother grocery shopping at a nearby supermarket, that was a big mistake. Because once I got inside, I had a panic attack. I rushed to my mother and said, "I have to leave. I'm feeling sick." My head was spinning like a top. I was so dizzy. I had survived heart palpitations. My mother stopped getting her groceries, and we rushed to the checkout counter, where I felt safe and could escape those feelings. It was difficult for me to walk up and down the aisles in a supermarket for a long time. I felt like I was suffocating. I couldn't breathe. When I stopped driving after the grocery incident, my niece Louise drove my mother and me around to different places.

I knew my mother wanted me to live a happy, normal life. No mother likes to see their child suffering from a mental illness that is overwhelming and emotionally exhausting. It wasn't like I was having a physical problem and she could give me medication to solve the problem. One day, out of the blue, my mother came up with a solution to help solve some of my problems. Believe me when I tell you, my mother helped me with my problem more than any psychiatrist I had seen.

I had not been driving for a while, and my mother could see I was getting deeper and deeper into depression. I knew my mother, along with my family, were praying for me. But my mother went a little further the day Louise took us shopping at the mall. My mother was in her late eighties, and she loved shopping at the mall. She didn't let any grass grow under her feet. Whenever she had plans to go somewhere, she would be ready to leave early. Soon after we got to the mall, I got sick.

I said to my mother, "I need to sit down to get some rest because I am getting dizzy, and I can't breathe." My mother said, "No, you don't need to sit down. You can do it." Occasionally, my mother would look at Louise while talking to me. I didn't learn until later that she had told Louise not to feel sorry for me if I asked her to take me home. Every time I would go out with my mother and Louise, I noticed they wouldn't let me rest or take me home when I said I was sick. I was so angry because I thought they didn't believe me. I knew my mother loved me, and she would never treat me that way. I really couldn't figure out why she was so hard on me. The only time my mother had been that hard on me was when I was younger and did childish things. I thought, *my mother doesn't care about the way I feel. Why is she so mean to me?* Little did I know she was helping me. What my mother did to me that day turned out to be a blessing in disguise.

I didn't learn until later that my mother was trying to help me. She said, "I told Louise not to pity you because if we did, you wouldn't try to help yourself." It worked. Because at that moment, when I was so angry with her, I didn't focus on the panic attack. I felt like she and Louise didn't care how badly I was suffering. I later realized I'd done exactly what my mother wanted me to do. She used reverse psychology to help snap me out of my self-pity by replacing fear with anger. Before I realized what was happening, I could walk around the mall without fearing a panic attack. I forgot all about the strange feelings I was experiencing.

I had gained enough courage to fight the fear. It was a miracle. I blocked the panic attack from escalating. I was not afraid anymore. My thought process was to not let fear control me by showing my mother and Louise that I don't need their help. I used the moral anger method to overcome fear while I remained silent. Although anger can cause you to get into trouble many times, I felt my anger was appropriate. In retrospect, there was a positive outcome of my mother's actions. Otherwise, I probably would never go to a mall again in my life without proper help.

For a while, when I went shopping, I would say to myself, "I'll show my mother. I don't need her to pity me." I forgot all about those strange feelings. The reverse psychology my mother used on me helped. Now I can go to the mall and supermarket without panicking. Praise God for the help of my mother. I know there are different methods people having panic attacks used to conquer their fears. But repeating my mother's powerful words—"you can do it"—worked for me.

When Louise got a job and could no longer drive us around, my mother looked at me and said, "I guess you are going to have to drive." I thought she was joking until I saw the serious look on her face. Before I responded, I thought my mother must be out of her mind. I said, "I can't drive." My mother just ignored what I said. She did not take no for an answer. She said, "How do you know you can't drive? You should at least try it." My mother insisted that I drive to the supermarket because it was a short drive that took only a few minutes.

The fear had me thinking I couldn't do it. But my mother's words convinced me once again, "You can do it." I got enough courage and said to my mother, "I will try." Before I got inside the car, I said a prayer. "God, please help me. I can't keep living like this." I will admit, I was a nervous wreck. All the while I was driving, my mother repeatedly said, "You can do it." I noticed my mother watching me as I parked the car at the supermarket with a smile on her face. I knew what that meant. She was just as relieved as I was. I had driven the car without having a panic attack. My mother said, "I told you that you could do it."

I can't tell you how happy I was to be driving again without having a panic attack. It took a while before I got over the fear of driving a car, but I didn't let it stop me. Every time I felt a panic attack trying to take control, I took a deep breath. And my mother would say, "You can do it." Those powerful words encouraged me to drive my car again, just like they helped me conquer my fear when I shopped at the mall and supermarket.

...

It broke my heart when I wasn't there for my daughter during her golden high school years. It made me sad I was disabled. And the fear of driving affected all aspects of my life. I couldn't take my daughter to different places like most parents. Thank God, I could depend on her friends' parents to take her to school activities during her freshman and sophomore years. The burden on my shoulders lifted somewhat when my daughter got her license and could drive my car to school during her junior and senior years.

When my daughter became drum major, she had to travel a lot to take part in competitions. I felt guilty I couldn't support my daughter and go on trips with the band to places like New York and Florida. I especially felt bad I couldn't participate when the school needed parents to help chaperone those trips.

It was tough for my daughter to cope with just one parent when her father passed away. She knew he would have been there for her in my absence if he were still alive. Although she was nine years old when he died, they were very close. Dave, my husband's best friend, visited often after he first died, and he told us how much he loved her and talked about her to him.

He nicknamed her "Baby Cake." I knew her father would have been just like my mother when he understood the whole truth about the panic attacks I was experiencing. He would have pressured me to start back driving like he did the day I drove him to his job. That was one thing I admired about my late husband; he had faith that I could do it.

When my daughter was old enough and could fully understand my experience with panic attacks, I felt comfortable talking to her about my problem. She observed me having lots of panic attacks. To my surprise, my daughter was just like my mother. She showed no pity when I had a panic attack. Instead, she wouldn't let the panic attack control me. One day, I had a panic attack while eating dinner at the kitchen table. I suddenly lost control. I got up and stood in the corner. My daughter noticed what was happening. I thought she would be afraid and call my mother or 911. Instead, she whispered, "Mama, don't move. Just continue taking deep breaths. What are you afraid of?" I was still shaking. She took me in her arms to console me. Then she said, "Mommy, you are letting those panic attacks control you. You've got to fight back. When you have one, stand still and talk back to that fear." My daughter and my mother were telling me the same thing. When I had a panic attack and my daughter was around, she did not let fear control me. She was very demanding. She chanted, "No, Mommy. What did I tell you? You can do it." I would listen to her and do the breathing exercises she said to do. I would take a deep breath and breathe out slowly. I did it until I calmed down. I don't know how she knew what to do, but doing those exercises worked for me. And repeating those powerful words—you can do it—was working like a dose of medicine. Later, I realized that the nurse with the African accent had said the same thing when I went to the hospital. "I can do it." I didn't want my daughter to see me that way. She needed me. I had no other choice but to fight to overcome the fear for myself and for my daughter.

 I remember I was going to church for an evening service, driving across a short bridge. I was so anxious and nervous. My daughter was with me. She didn't have a license at the time. My daughter tried to interact with the fear by talking the whole time I was driving. I said I couldn't do this. I would never drive across that bridge again. My daughter replied, "How will you get to church then?"

 "I will take another route."

 "No, Mommy. You can't do that. If you go the longer route, it will take you longer to get to church. You don't need to do that. You are running away from your fear."

 I knew she was right. It was like my daughter and my mother were working together, trying to help me drive again. They both told me the same thing, "You can do it." I wanted to make my daughter proud. So, I took her advice. It wasn't easy to drive across that bridge alone. When my daughter or mother was with me when I drove, some of the fear was easy to overcome because they would talk to me.

 Although it took me a while to gain confidence to drive across the bridge, I never gave up hope I could do it. I noticed keeping the radio sort of loud and singing along with the songs helped ease some of my fear. After driving across the bridge for a while and repeating the words "I can do it," I gained the confidence to drive across the bridge with no problems. Sometimes, I forget I am driving across the bridge because I learned not to let that monster take control of me.

 I learned from those experiences that I let monsters control me, just like I did that night he raped me. I didn't fight back the fear. While I was being raped, I just laid there and accepted what was happening because I was afraid that I would die. That's what happens when you have a panic attack. You become so afraid during the episode that you become so paralyzed by fear and feel as though you are going to die. The valuable lesson I learned from my mother and daughter was that no matter what you go through, let nothing control you. You have the power to fight back. And once you fight back, that fear will vanish. Also, I sincerely believe that's why God gave me the scripture to repeat every day: He did not give me the spirit of fear, but of power, love, and a sound mind. I thank God he gave my daughter and mother the courage to help me regain the ability to drive and shop at the mall and supermarket. I don't remember when it happened, but soon after I conquered my fear of driving a car, I could sit at the front of the church. I could sit anywhere I wanted to. I was making progress with my mother's help. We had moved to another sanctuary by then, and it was twice as large as the old church, which was a good thing. I didn't feel like I was being smothered. Just before my mother had a special seat on the Mother's Board, I could sit in the front of the sanctuary with her.

Looking back, Ms. Anderson was right. My daughter and family were my moral support because without their help, I don't think I would have gotten that far.

28

My Daughter Frees Me

I had two hurdles to conquer: riding in a car and driving a car. My daughter was grateful that I overcame the fear of driving. But I still had the fear of riding in a car when someone else was driving, especially riding long distance. My daughter was determined that I was going to ride in a car. She said, "You've gotten over the fear you couldn't drive. I know you can get over the fear of riding in a car."

I was so proud of my daughter when she said, "Don't worry, Mommy. I can drive. I'll follow my friend Crystal's mother to college." Like most parents, I wanted to be the one dropping my daughter off for her first year of college on her move-in day. I felt sad because my panic attacks made me miss out on so many things for her.

My daughter had been driving for only two years and had never driven that distance before. She became nervous about driving three hours alone to the University of North Carolina-Greensboro (UNCG) for the first time. It terrified her. Fortunately, she was not like me. She didn't let fear deter her.

When I was experiencing the feeling of empty-nest syndrome, I depended on my mother. The day my daughter left for college, I cried. We were so close. I could always depend on my daughter. She never gave me any problems. One day we went shopping, and while she was paying for her item, the cashier asked if we were sisters. My daughter liked the idea that I looked as young as she did, but she didn't want to look as old as me. I was in my late fifties. When her father died, I had to be the father and mother. One day, my mother told me she noticed my daughter mimicking everything I do. She teased and said, "You better be careful what you do, because Dee tries to do everything you do." I made sure I did positive things. When I became an usher and choir member in the church, so did she.

I stopped ushering; my daughter did so as well. When she started dating, I immediately talked to her about the birds and the bees. Also, it was important to me to let her know how a man should treat a woman. I taught her that education was essential. She always abided by those rules. She knew after she ate supper, she had to do homework. She often teased her friends that I never had to spank her because she was a good girl. To be honest, she was always mature.

I often told her she had been here before. No matter what I was going through, I always gave her a birthday party every year until she was sixteen years old. I remember when she turned seven years old; I had a clown at her party. Neither my daughter nor her guests were excited. No matter how many tricks the clown did, they just sat there like it was no big deal. My daughter told me the clown was not that funny. "A waste of money," I said to my husband.

My mother and I needed each other for comfort. Both our husbands had passed away. Not a day went by that we were not at each other's houses. Before my mother passed away, I spent every night with her. She was in her nineties. My siblings and I didn't want her to stay alone, especially at nighttime. My daughter was at ease knowing I had started driving again, and I didn't have to depend on her to take me places like she'd done before she left for college. My mother was just as happy. She no longer had to worry about someone else taking her places—most of all, to church and the supermarket.

...

I didn't know how many miles Greensboro was from my hometown, but I knew it was about a three-hour drive. No matter how much I tried not to contemplate a panic attack before I got into the car, I just couldn't fight that monster. I always sat in the back seat with a cover over my head when riding a long distance. My daughter talked to me as she drove to Greensboro. She wanted to take my mind off having a panic attack. Occasionally, my daughter said, "Do you want me to stop someplace for a few minutes so you can get yourself together?" I didn't want to stop. I wanted to get there as fast as I could. I just needed to compose myself.

My daughter didn't take no for an answer when I told her I didn't think I could take that long ride. She acted the same way when she helped me conquer my fear in my kitchen that day. She said, "Don't let the panic attack define who you are. If you fought the fear of driving a car, you can fight the fear of riding in a car." I knew my daughter was right. I had come too far to turn around. I thought, *I can do it.*

I gathered enough courage to go to my daughter's college because I wanted to see the campus, her dorm room, and meet her roommates. Once I saw how small the dorm room she was sharing with her roommate was, I was happy she moved into the residence hall. She had more privacy. It was like a four-room apartment she shared with four other students. There were two baths, a kitchen, and a living room.

While my daughter was attending college at UNCG and the University of North Carolina School of the Arts (UNC Winston-Salem), she would come and get me to visit her at least two or three times a year. No matter how many times she wanted me to go, I refused. Thank God when she got her doctorate at UNC-Chapel Hill; she took online classes. I didn't have to worry about going to visit her. The only time I went to the school was the day she graduated. And the ride was not as long and miserable as the other colleges she attended.

My daughter would not give up on me riding in a car. She was determined that one day I could do it without having a panic attack. I felt bad not going with her. Although I knew it would be a miserable ride, I took the trips to please her. What encouraged me to go was when my daughter would say to me, "You can do it." I remember those were my mother's famous words. It took a while to relieve some of the fear before I felt comfortable riding in a car. I persevered, knowing that one day I was going to overcome that monster.

I had a fear of visiting my daughter when she got married and moved to Raleigh. It was closer to me than the ride to her college, just about an hour and a half ride. When I was in the car on my way to visit her and felt myself triggering a panic attack, I just said those powerful words, "I can do it." It took some time, but I gained enough courage to fight the fear. I wouldn't let it prevent me from seeing my daughter and grandchildren. My daughter was so proud of how I had enough courage to fight to overcome the fear of riding to and from Raleigh. Most of the time, I didn't even contemplate having an attack. If I felt the tired feeling about to appear, I'd just repeat, "I can do it," and ignore the monster.

With the help of my daughter and by persevering, I can now take those long trips to Greensboro and Winston-Salem without worrying about having a panic attack. I'm so happy I didn't give up. Although I haven't driven long distances for more than an hour on the highway, it is not that I am fearful of having a panic attack. Now that I am older, I don't like driving in heavy traffic driving faster than 55mph. When I stay with my daughter in Raleigh, she or my son-in-law will drive my car to her house. Thank God, I can drive on the main streets in town to any place I want to go without having a panic attack. Every time I drive or ride in a car, I have a smile on my face and raise my head toward the sky and tell God, "Thank You, I can do it". The feeling I have is like I hit the lottery for millions of dollars. It's a joy I can go alone shopping at the supermarket, malls, doctor, or any other place I want to go. For so many years, I prayed for this day and God has answered my prayers.

Quite a few times, I have taken trips with my daughter and my son-in-law, Ted, to places like South Carolina, Georgia, and Florida. Sometimes I had to fight the fear, but it was nothing like before. I use my powerful words, "I can do it."

I realize now that my experience with panic attack disorder was something I should have dealt with years ago, before it got out of hand. But the progress I made has put me in a place I never thought I'd be. And I know my mother is looking down from heaven with a big smile on her face, saying, "You can do it." I no longer have to write in my journal, telling God about my secret and asking Him to please help me. But I give Him thanks for the good days and not the miserable life I was experiencing.

...

I heard so many people talk about visiting the National Museum of African American History and Culture in Washington, D.C. And it was a nice place to visit to learn about the richness and diversity of African American history and culture. When I got the chance to go, I had doubts about riding the bus. I still hadn't recovered from the first episode I experienced while riding the bus when I worked at the telephone company. Although I was getting a lot better at being in a car, it had been a while since I rode a bus. The last time was in the early 1990s. They invited my former pastor and the church members to render a service at his former church in Baltimore. I went because I wanted to take my daughter. It had been a while since she had taken a long-distance trip other than going to Busch Gardens.

The entire trip was a miserable ride. I was anxious about having a panic attack before I got on the bus. I was a nervous wreck. The bus was packed, and I couldn't breathe. Of course, I didn't want anyone to know I couldn't ride a bus. I somehow hid those strange feelings by covering my head with a blanket on the way to and from Baltimore.

As I was boarding the bus to Washington, D.C., I felt a little nervous when I saw the bus was at capacity. I made sure I didn't sit near people I knew just in case of a panic attack. When my sister Bell wanted me to sit near her and her husband, William, I refused. It was not because I didn't want to sit near her. I wanted to sit in the back, just in case I had an episode. I was so happy my nephew Darnell was sitting in the back when he saw me looking for a place to sit. He said, "Aunt Mary, you can sit with me." He took his two children, Henry and Jane. They named Jane after my late mother. We all sat in the back having fun. That made the time go by fast. When we got closer to Washington, D.C., we took lots of pictures of different historic buildings. And I didn't have any problem all the way there.

But on the way back, I again feared a panic attack. I don't know what could have triggered an attack unless it was the heavy traffic. I was so proud of myself when I fought back by having faith in God to help me. I whispered a prayer. I said, "God, I can't deal with this. You have to take control because I am going to sleep. I will not let this monster take control of me." I knew God answered my prayer. I covered my head with my small blanket and said, "I can do it." Within a few minutes, I was fast asleep. When I woke up, we were back in North Carolina.

29 Robert

The choir was singing a beautiful song that caught my attention. When I looked at the lead singer, I didn't recognize who he was at first. All the pews in the front were full of people. That blocked my view because I was sitting in the back of the church. I recognized who he was when I could see clearly. It shocked me to see him. I thought I would never see him again in my life. That moment triggered a flashback to that night he raped me. I could barely sit in my seat comfortably and struggled to breathe. My heart was palpitating as I emotionally relived that night. I was losing control, screaming inside just like when it happened. I wanted to leave immediately. I leaned over and whispered into my daughter's ear, saying, "I want to go home." She didn't have a clue why I wanted to leave so suddenly. My daughter thought I was sick. When we got inside the car, she realized I was having a panic attack. Immediately, she helped me with the breathing in and out exercise; she taught me to compose myself. As I calmed down, that's when I explained to her why I had to leave so abruptly. My daughter was just as shocked as I was when I said the lead singer was the guy who raped me. I am grateful that I spoke to my daughter about the night I was sexually assaulted because it would have been challenging for me to explain my reactions at church that Sunday evening. Although I had fully recovered from having panic attacks in church, that one was bound to happen. It didn't matter where I would have been when I saw him. I would have lost control.

I wanted to go to the evening service because most church members had planned to support the pastor. He had been invited to preach at another church for their pastor's anniversary service. My daughter went with me because she was home from college for several days. And she was still a member of the church.

When my daughter learned I was a victim of sexual assault, it was one of the most challenging conversations I'd ever had with her. I didn't know how it would affect her. I told her when I felt she was mature enough to understand. She was distraught, as I'd known she would be. I noticed we both had tears in our eyes when I said he threatened me with a gun. I was so frightened when he said he would kill me if I didn't obey his command. Just like my parents, my daughter was asking questions about him I couldn't answer. I said the incident left me so traumatized, I couldn't remember the date, the year, or the day it happened. I didn't remember the make and color of the car. My daughter felt some comfort when she learned how I could repress that night by watching one of Oprah Winfrey's shows on sexual assault victims. She was relieved to know that I stopped blaming myself and I could talk about the assault without feeling guilty.

I had been suffering from fear for years about that night. My daughter said, "Mommy, I believe the traumatic experience is the reason you suffered from those intense feelings of distress and fear. This may be what causes your panic attacks." My daughter felt the best way for me to deal with that night was to get closure. She was right, because once you become a victim of sexual assault, it will haunt you until you die. I found it difficult to accept that he was never punished. My parents did the best they could, trying to have him punished. The only thing they could do was to sweep it under the rug. After what happened to me, it was important to my parents that my brothers knew the meaning of consent. And they firmly believed that no woman should be taken advantage of. When my two brothers were older, I noticed they took my parents' advice because they treated women with dignity and respect by following in my father's footsteps.

When my daughter turned the ignition on in the car, she couldn't drive fast enough to get away from the church. Seeing Robert again totally caught me off guard. Later, I learned he had moved back home after living up north for years. I did not know what had happened to him. He was the last person I would have wanted to stay in contact with. I saw Robert unexpectedly for the second time when his church was a guest at my church for an afternoon service. Once again, I panicked. It wasn't until later that I learned he was a member of the guest church. Had I known, I would have left before the guest church arose.

As I observed the guests walking into church on the opposite side from where I was sitting, Robert rushed at breakneck speed, going to the choir stand. It appeared he was late. All the choir members were seated before him. I was surprised to see him again. Just being in the same place with a person who sexually assaulted you … It's hard to explain how I felt. It sparked a panic attack. I was losing control. I did not want to be in his presence. I couldn't contain myself. I had to leave right away. I whispered to my friend Maxine and said, "I don't want to be in the same place with that guy over there. I have to leave." She had no clue what I was talking about. I said I would talk to her later, grabbed my belongings, and rushed out of the church as fast as possible to get into my car. The whole time I was driving, I couldn't hold back the tears welling up in my eyes. It was difficult to control my emotions and drive. It was like all the fear and anguish exploding inside me at the same time. For years, I had carried a heavy burden on my shoulders, and I felt he had turned my life into a living nightmare.

Although I was uncomfortable seeing Robert again, I knew it would only be a matter of time. I would probably be in his presence on some occasions. I lived in a small town where everybody knows everybody personally or through a mutual friend. Often, I'd go to the grocery store and run into someone I knew. My family and classmates also attended most of the churches I attended in the surrounding areas.

Later that evening, I called Maxine to explain why I'd left so abruptly. I knew I could talk to her about my problem because she was just like a part of my family. I appreciated she was supportive when I explained to her about that night. And she was not judgmental like some of my cousins, who'd said it was my fault.

When I stopped at the restaurant to get takeout, I saw Robert once again. He was the last person I wanted to see after a stressful day at school. When I resigned from my position as church clerk after nineteen years of service, I went back to school. I felt it was the perfect time to earn the degree I'd dreamed of having fifty-two years ago. For a long time, my daughter had tried to convince me to go back to school. I procrastinated because I thought I was too old.

But choosing to continue my education was a great goal. In the beginning, it was kind of scary being older than the teachers and students in all my classes. But it soon faded away when I noticed there were just as many older adults in college as the young.

The only embarrassing moment I had at school was when I had a severe panic attack in my public speaking class. A panic attack would emerge when I was in stressful situations, like when I was taking an exam or speaking in class. However, many people experience stress or anxiety before an exam. Still, it was so excessive that it interfered with my performance when I took an exam. My teachers gave me extra time to reduce the possibility of having panic attacks, which helped a lot.

Also, I felt I stressed myself out studying hard the night before the speech because I wanted to earn an A, which I did. I got only one C, which was good, especially at sixty-five years old. All I remember that day was going to my seat after finishing my speech. Suddenly, I felt light-headed and dizzy. Before I realized what was happening, everything turned dark. I couldn't see. I didn't know I had fainted until I came to. The teacher and students came to my rescue and told me what had happened. They were so frightened. They thought I was dying. The paramedic that the school called examined me, but I chose not to go to the hospital. I had my sister take me to the nearest doctor, and I was fine. Just like I knew I would be. Stress and being in a packed room with the door closed were what had triggered the panic attack. I had trouble with breathing the moment I began my speech, along with heart palpitations. My hands were sweaty, and I needed air. My classmates said I kept saying I needed some air as I reached for the door just before I fainted.

The first day I walked into my public speaking classroom and noticed how small and tightly packed the room was, I just brushed it off, thinking I wouldn't have a problem. However, I knew claustrophobia had an extreme effect on me. Being in closed places had caused me to have panic attacks for years. I thought I could handle it after I had spoken several times in class with no problem. And most of the time, I wasn't in class for a full hour. We mostly did our homework and tests online.

When I babysat my oldest grandchild, Tommy, before he went to daycare, I went to class online. I did homework and took my tests online at night. One night when I had to take my math test, I was sitting in the playroom with both doors closed. My daughter had just purchased the house. As I was sitting in the room, a nervous wreck taking the test, I had an episode of claustrophobia.

I immediately opened the door to get some air. For a while, I did not go into the playroom with the door closed. When I told my daughter I felt like I was suffocating in her playroom, she said, "Turn on the fan, open the doors, or go to another room." I kept the fan on and opened the door as she said. But I didn't stop taking tests in the playroom. I was determined to overcome that fear. I knew that was the kids' playroom, and I was determined to sit in there with them. I listened to my daughter when she said, "Mommy, if you overcame the fear of riding in a car, I know you can sit in the playroom." She was right. I told myself, I can do it. I knew I would visit my daughter and sometimes spend the nights—I could not let one room in her house deter me. First, I tried sitting in the playroom with the doors open and turning on the fan. I continued to say, "I can do it." Not only can I go into the playroom with the kids to play, but I sit in there as long as I want and watch TV. My daughter was so amazed to see how far I had come in overriding my fear. Sometimes I'd sit in the playroom and think, *I remember the first time I came in here, I thought I was going to pass out. But now, thank God, the fear has vanished.*

...

It had been years since I had a severe panic attack. I didn't see it coming. I had read somewhere that many people get very nervous speaking in public. It can be more fearful than death. The first time I spoke at church, I felt the same way as I did in class. I had a panic attack. But once I went outside to get some air, I started to regain my strength. I didn't let that incident stop me. I conquered the fear and continued speaking in churches.

I didn't do much cooking while I was in school. I would go to the restaurant to get takeout. When I stopped at the restaurant, I spotted Robert standing about ten feet away from me. This was the third time I had seen him. Every time I saw him, I relived the fear I felt when he pointed a gun at my face.

I rushed to get my food. I wanted to get out of there as fast as I could. As I was walking out of the restaurant, Robert was standing near a table talking to someone. I had no other choice but to pass by him when I exited the restaurant. It was one way in and one way out. I tried to keep my distance from him. I did not want to look into his face. I had my head down, walking as fast as I could. I slowly raised my head when I thought I heard Robert say, "Hello."

I stared at him with a surprised look on my face. Once again, I was afraid. I couldn't speak. The nerve of this guy, I thought. I didn't know what to do, so I kept walking as fast as I could toward my car. I was nervous and angry. When I got home, I called my daughter. "I saw Robert in the restaurant today after class, and I was uncomfortable being around him. How dare he speak to me as if nothing happened? Doesn't he know he ruined my life?"

My daughter said, "Mommy, maybe you should have talked to him and let him know how he has affected your life."

At first, I didn't know how to respond to my daughter. I pondered what she said. It took some time for me to agree with her because I was afraid of what might happen. I said, "Maybe you're right. I need to let him know that what he did to me has made my life a living hell." I needed some closure. It's difficult to confront someone who has assaulted you. For me, I wanted him to be just as miserable as I had been. I wanted him punished for what he'd done to me.

Closure and Forgiveness

Sometimes I ask this question: If someone hurt you so badly and the fear never goes away, what would you do? Would you forgive them? I struggled with forgiveness the last time I saw Robert.

The only places I would see Robert were at church or my favorite restaurant. I remember it was May 2018, when I was in his presence for the last time. I will never forget that day as long as I live. I had just left class. I was so excited that I had finally returned to PCC and would soon receive my degree after fifty-two years. I was so proud of all the accomplishments I had achieved. I received an award for being a part of the second class in 1966 to integrate PCC. I was overjoyed with the hard work I put into studying, and I finished with a 3.6 GPA.

When I first attended PCC in 1966, I had high hopes of finishing in two years to become a secretary. I remember the first day I attended. I felt both excited and nervous. It was my first time attending school with Black and White students. In 1954, the Supreme Court ruled unanimously that racial segregation for children in public schools was unconstitutional. *Brown v. Board of Education* was a major cornerstone of the civil rights movement. After the Civil Rights Act was passed in 1964, I remember so well that it prohibited discrimination in public places and required integration of employment and schools. I was overwhelmed when I saw myself on TV sitting at the lunchroom table with my friends when the news reporter came to do a story on integration. There were significant strides made toward desegregation, and it was challenging. I was proud to be part of the second class to integrate PCC in 1966.

The Vernon E. White Building was the only building then, and that was where I had all my classes. All my teachers were White, and I wasn't used to being taught by White teachers. But that didn't affect the teachers' relationship with the Black or White students. I cannot recall if there were ever any incidents with the students or teachers. Although there were Black and White students in class together, we were still segregated. The environment was not the same for Blacks sitting in the class together with White students. After all, it had only been two years since the Civil Rights Act was passed. The Black students felt most comfortable being together in the classroom. That's why the Blacks students sat on one side of the room and the White students sat on the other.

    I embraced my potential to become a secretary after I had fallen in love with typing. That was one of my favorite subjects. No matter how hard I tried, it took me a while to gain my typing speed without looking at the keyboard. Back in the day, I used a manual typewriter. They had not yet invented electric typewriters. Every week, the teacher would give an A to the student who typed twenty-five words or more per minute. My friend was an excellent typist. Most of the time, she would type over twenty-five words per minute. I wanted to type fast like my friend. One day, I saw this beautiful brown typewriter in an Alden order book for $13.00. I took it upon myself to order it without my parents' permission. I got in trouble, and my father returned the typewriter the same day it was delivered. He didn't have the money to pay for it. Of course, it broke my heart, but I was determined to reach my goal. So many days, I would sit at the kitchen table and pretend it was my imaginary typewriter keyboard. My typing speed improved. I finished high school typing thirty-five words per minute. That was the requirement back then to be qualified as a good typist. I made my teacher proud.

    It was my early ambition to join the army after I graduated from high school. I wanted to travel, and it would help toward my college education. When I was told I did not meet their criteria because I was underweight, I applied to attend Pitt Community College.

    It wasn't easy for my mother to struggle and sacrifice to send me to school. I remember how hard I cried that day toward the end of my first year of school, when my mother said she could no longer borrow money to pay for my tuition. My dream of becoming a secretary just flushed down the drain right in front of my face. Every quarter, my mother borrowed a portion of my thirty-four-dollar tuition. Never mind the other expenses. Back then, thirty-four dollars was a lot of money. I couldn't have attended school if it hadn't been for the White lady she worked for during the summer loaning her the money.

When summer came, my mother paid back the money by working on the lady's farm. She barely had enough money left over to help support the family. My parents were not sharecroppers, but the only seasonal income was working on the farms during the summer. My parents had their children's best interests in mind. They wanted us to go to college, but they could not afford it. Grants and student loans were something my parents did not know existed.

The only job for Black people during the summer back then was farm work. I didn't want to work on the farm like my parents. It was dirty and brutal work. Plus, the pay would not be enough money to cover my tuition and other school expenses. My mother was just as concerned about me going back to school as I was. I knew the only way to continue going to school was to get a job other than farm work to earn enough money to pay for tuition. The only way I could do that, I had to go up north. At the time, my father had a job working at a restaurant in Washington, D.C. And he tried to get me a job working with him. My father worked there temporarily to make enough money to support the family. There were few jobs available for Black people once the farm work was completed for the year. Most of the Black men in my community traveled to Florida and Tennessee to work temporarily in the tobacco market. Then they sent money back home to support their families. I remember every week my mother would go to the post office to get the twenty-dollar money order that my father mailed to her to support the family. When my father said his boss had hired me, I didn't worry about going back to school anymore. I knew I would make enough money to graduate the following year. I was like a fish out of the water when my father came home to get me to take me back with him. Patricia and I arrived in Washington, D.C., around the same time. I knew her from high school. She had just graduated and come there to look for employment. We stayed together in the same apartment. We went looking for a job at the same restaurant where her father and my father worked.

I didn't know what to expect when the boss hired Patricia and not me. After all, he knew my father had taken a trip home to get me to work there. When Patricia and I went to the restaurant to work, the boss put Patricia to work right away, bussing tables. He left me sitting at a table for almost an hour, saying nothing to me. Finally, I said to my father, "Do you know why the boss has not talked to me yet?" My father went into the boss's office to talk to him. It was like a slap in the face when my father said the boss would not hire me. He said there were no more openings. I didn't know what to say. I just stood there in the restaurant with tears welling in my eyes. I had gone to Washington, D.C., with high hopes of getting a job to continue going to PCC. But just like that, I had no job. My father said, "I will get to the bottom of this." It wasn't until later my father was told that Patricia's father told the boss not to hire me because I was ill with kidney disease. I am sure he overheard his daughter Patricia having a conversation about when I went to see the doctor. He didn't hear the entire conversation. If he had, he would have known I'd said the doctor told me to drink plenty of water to prevent a kidney infection. I never had a kidney condition. Until this day, I believe Patricia's father told that lie to secure a job for his daughter in case I got hired first.

I probably would have gotten a job if I had stayed in Washington, D.C., a while longer, but my mother felt that my father and I should come home. I did not argue with her. I didn't like Washington, D.C. There was a lot of crime in the area. I remember the first couple of days after I arrived there, someone was murdered around the corner from where I stayed. I was so afraid. I was not used to that kind of living. I planned to stay long enough to earn enough money during the summer to go back to school in the fall.

When my father and I were riding in the taxi on our way to the bus station to go back home, it was at that moment I realized I was not going back to school the following year. I had no money. But I never gave up hope of returning to school. I was determined to obtain a degree one day. That's what my focus was on that day I saw Robert in the restaurant. I was so proud that in a couple of months, I would be graduating. It was a dream come true. Soon after I saw Robert, all my happiness went down the drain. Immediately, I remembered what my daughter said to do if I ever ran into him again. I needed to confront him about that dreadful night and gain closure.

I had to do it. Time was running out. I'd made up my mind I would confront him about that night if I saw him again. I didn't want him to leave before I could talk to him. It was like I had an adrenaline rush and a fight-or-flight response simultaneously. I thought, *Today, Robert will hear what I have to say*. Before I could say anything to him, he spoke to me.

Robert said, "You are Bishop Parker's sister, ain't you?" Robert was in my younger brother's class. I didn't answer him. *How dare he ask me that stupid question?* He knew who I was. I was not about to let him think he could start a conversation with me about my brother and brush off what happened that night. I gave him an angry look. All my fears were gone. I said, "Can I talk to you for a moment?" He followed me outside the restaurant.

I said, "I am sure you know why every time you speak or say something to me, I don't respond. How dare you act like you didn't rape me? I know you don't expect me to act like nothing happened that night. You took something from me I was unwilling to give you, and I have been suffering for years. You don't know what I have been thinking over the past fifty-some years. I have never gotten over that night." Every time he tried to say something, I cut him off. I was not about to let him take control of me like he did that night. I was in control. I was holding the gun in his face like he did to me. I wanted him to know what he did to me had affected my life for over fifty-four years. He needed to know I'd been frightened when he put a gun in my face and threatened to kill me if I didn't obey his commands.

I heard later from some of my cousins that the gun was not real. Robert didn't say if it was real or not. He knew that in the dark, no one could tell the difference.

I could tell Robert was uncomfortable reliving that night. He kept interrupting me while I was talking a mile a minute. He said, "I am so sorry. Will you please forgive me?" I paused for a second when he asked for forgiveness. I was shocked because I hadn't expected an apology. However, I continued talking. I could not accept an apology. I just couldn't do it. I was still angry because he was never punished. I knew Robert was waiting for me to accept his apology. I was not ready. Repeatedly, he apologized.

He said that he had been through some tough times and that he had changed. God had come into his life, and he was now a minister.

I didn't want to hear about his life. I wanted him to know that he took control of my body without my consent. He had gotten away with an impurity. I walked back into the restaurant to place my order. He asked if he could pay for my food. I said, "No, thank you." He begged. "Please let me pay for your food. I am so sorry for what I did. At least let me pay for it." I said, "No." He gave the cashier the money. I could not eat the food. I didn't want anything from him. I couldn't look into his face any longer. I just wanted to go home. I left him standing outside the restaurant.

He repeatedly said, "Forgive me," as I was walking to my car. I admit I could feel a weight being lifted off my shoulders as I was driving away. Unfortunately, no matter how hard he apologized, he could not erase the fear, panic attacks, or anything I had gone through over those many years.

That evening, my son-in-law picked me up to take me to Raleigh to his house to babysit. When we arrived at the house, I greeted my daughter and right away I told her about the conversation I'd had with Robert at the restaurant. She was speechless. She cried profusely. My son-in-law was distraught too. That was the first time he had heard of the rape. He couldn't say a word. It was like we had left a sad funeral. My daughter hugged me. She held me for a long time. She said, "Mommy, are you okay?" I couldn't say I was okay, but it was a relief to let Robert know how I had suffered for so many years. My daughter felt I did the right thing and hoped I would have a sense of closure. I know it will take some time to digest what I had to do, as that night will forever haunt me.

...

As I tell my story, I can't help but think about Dr. Ford. I pray she can get some closure. If the person who assaulted you admits what they did, perhaps that would relieve some of the tension. It's bad enough that you carry that burden on your shoulders for years. But when the person says, "I don't know you," or "It never happened," that's a hard pill to swallow. One thing you must remember is do not blame yourself.

It's not our fault that someone did not have the decency to understand that no means no! My prayers will forever be with her and other victims that have gotten no closure.

For years, I went through hell and high water about that night.

When you face the person who raped you, you don't know how to act. As I spoke to Robert, I remembered everything about that night, but I didn't have a panic attack!

I am sure the anger that had built up in me overrode those feelings. I heard my daughter's and my mother's voices as they assured me I had it under control. "You can do it," they said. They were right!

I am a Christian, and I prayed to God to help me accept Robert's apology. I have read in the Bible if God can forgive us, then we must forgive our brothers and sisters. I will tell you it's tough to forgive when someone hurts you so badly and leaves a scar that will haunt you for the rest of your life. I will admit, it wasn't easy for me to forgive. After doing some soul searching, praying, and the teaching I was taught about forgiveness in Bible study, I forgave him. I realized if I didn't forgive Robert, I would forever carry the monster on my shoulder that I had struggled with for so many years. I wanted him punished for what he did to me. So, I had to release Robert to God and He will do to him what I couldn't do.

I believe it was God's will for me to confront him, to let him know how much I had suffered, because I have not seen him since our conversation at the restaurant. I thank God I am not the same person I was fifty-two years ago. I've been told God works in mysterious ways, and finally, he answered my prayers.

I also thank God that I have overcome the visible and invisible monster that had traumatized my life for years. Even though I didn't seek the proper help, I thank God for my mother and daughter pushing me not to give up. I thought I would never drive or ride in a car again. Let alone go shopping at the mall, supermarket, and going to church. As I mentioned, whenever I ride or drive, I look up to the sky and thank God that I have no fear of having a panic attack. Matter of fact, I don't even contemplate having a panic attack like in the past. I just enjoy the ride. In the near future, my daughter and I plan to take a trip. We will be flying. She said, "Do you think you can handle it?" "Of course I can," I replied. I have no fear or doubt that I can't do it. If I can ride in a car, bus, or train with no problem, why not a plane? Not only am I planning to fly, but to go back to school to get my bachelor's degree. I have to keep fighting. I won't give up. I will not let the invisible monster take over my life again. The key for me is not to let the monster win, no matter how hard it can be when you feel like your body is losing control and like you are going to die. Fight back and tell yourself you can do it. My mother's famous words.

My advice to anyone who suffers from panic attack disorder is not to give up. Don't let fear overwhelm you. Don't be ashamed to tell someone. Unlike me, a panic attack was unknown to me back in the day. That's why I suffered for so long. Even though the experience makes you feel like you're losing your mind or dying, don't let that stop you from seeking help. Unfortunately, at the time when I was suffering, most doctors didn't have a full understanding of how to treat panic attack disorder. And back then, it was unknown to most people.

Once you have been diagnosed by a mental health professional that you suffer from panic attack disorder, talk to your healthcare provider for the best treatment for you.

About the Author

Mary Sue Miller is a born-again Christian, lifelong faithful church member, a loving mother, and author. Mary's deep and personal relationship with God, reading and writing, and the guidance of the Holy Spirit have inspired Mary to write this book.

www.ingramcontent.com/pod-product-compliance
Lightning Source LLC
LaVergne TN
LVHW010220070526
838199LV00062B/4672